INTO THE VOID
Exploring the Mystery Between Death, Time, and Eternity

Renae C. Linde

An Independent Publication by CRF Luttrell

Expanded Distribution Edition © 2025 by Cynthia RF Luttrell

All rights reserved...

ISBN: 979-89990516-0-8

No portion of this book may be reproduced, stored, or transmitted in any form or by any means, electronic, mechanical, photocopying, recording, or otherwise, without the prior written permission from the copyright owner, except in the case of brief quotations embodied in reviews or articles as permitted by U.S. copyright law.

An Independent Publication by CRF Luttrell

CONTENTS

Introduction	1
PART I: BEFORE THE VOID	5
1. The Last Tick	7
2. What Is Null?	17
3. Time, Measured and Lost	29
4. The Eternal Blink	43
PART II: THROUGH THE VOID	57
5. The Void as Threshold	59
6. Consciousness Without Clockwork	71
7. When Memory Can't Follow	81
8. The Trouble with Knowing	93
PART III: BEYOND THE VOID	107
9. Preparing for the Blink	109
10. When the Clock Still Ticks for Others	121
Conclusion	131

References

INTRODUCTION

The Question That Won't Let Go

It begins quietly. Death doesn't announce itself. Something else happens first.

A moment when the rhythm of life fractures, subtly, irrevocably, and you realize you've been living as though time were a promise. It's as though the next breath was yours by right; as though the people you love are anchored here with you, indefinitely.

Then the thread snaps.

Not always loudly. Sometimes, it happens on an ordinary afternoon. You open the fridge. You scroll past a headline. You hear someone say, "He's gone," and the words enter your body like a foreign object. The calendar stays where it is. The sky doesn't shift, but something beneath the surface folds in on itself. You are no longer living in the same world.

Grief does this. So does age. Sometimes, wonder alone is enough. A starry sky that won't answer. A stillness too vast to fill. A body stilled in death, warm only moments ago. These moments don't offer explanations. They rupture sequence. They unsettle the scaffolding of story. They leave us with the unbearable question:

What happens between the last breath and forever?

Not only after death, but in it. In the space where someone slips from time into something else, or nothing. A blink. A crossing. A silence so complete it reshapes the air.

This book began there.

It does not present an argument, but a reckoning. I am not seeking to prove what cannot be proven, nor to comfort what ought to remain unsettled. I am seeking to dwell honestly with the dissonance. To ask, with reverence and without conclusion: Is death a true null, an absolute erasure of time, self, and meaning? Or is it a threshold, so immediate and ungraspable that our consciousness simply cannot register the crossing?

The question is old. We've named it through myth, through scripture, through physics. The river that ferries the dead. The trumpet that sounds in the twinkling of an eye. The slowing of time at the edge of a black hole. The Hebrew whisper that breath returns to God. The Greek imagination of wandering shadows. The psalmist's ache that "man is like a breath; his days are like a fleeting shadow."

Still, the void resists our reach.

So we build stories. We watch bedside monitors. We write songs. We whisper to those who've gone, as if they still occupy a corner of the world we just can't perceive. But beneath our rituals and metaphors lives the trembling sense that what we've lost isn't just presence, it's sequence. It's more than just their body, but their place in our time. Their rhythm in our days.

This is the grief we rarely name. The theological, psychological, existential unraveling that follows a single question:

Where did they go?

Not in spirit. Not in memory. In time.
This book will not answer that question. But it will keep asking. With science, with scripture, with story. With the full weight of unknowing. And maybe, by entering the silence between breath and eternity, we'll learn to listen differently.

Something is ending.

Or something is beginning.

And we are already leaning in.

Part 1: Before the Void

The Human Struggle to Grasp the End of Time

Chapter One
The Last Tick

The Question That Won't Let Go

A friend of mine buried her son on a Thursday and went back to work the following Monday. She certainly wasn't ready to return to work, but she didn't know what else to do. Her inbox was full. Her phone kept pinging. People needed her signature on documents and her opinion on vendor bids. She sat through meetings with swollen eyes and a sweatshirt from the back of her car.

She told me later that what shocked her most wasn't the silence at home or the absence of her son's shoes by the front door. It was how the world moved forward without friction. Nobody slowed down. The gas bill arrived. The lawn kept growing. She had to remember passwords, return emails, wash her hair.

Her youngest asked if they were still going on the spring break trip they'd planned months before. They didn't ask out of cruelty; they were just confused. There was a schedule on the fridge. The deposit had been paid. Did grief cancel everything, or only some things?

She said it felt like being stranded on a sidewalk while a parade marched past. It wasn't tragic; it was just loud and unbothered. It was like people tossing candy and a brass section playing something triumphant. Her life had cracked, but time refused to notice.

I remember sitting across from her at a diner two weeks after the funeral. She stirred her coffee, then said, "He's not even cold, and I still have to buy toilet paper."

That was the moment. Not when he died. Not the funeral. Not the condolences. That sentence. The blunt insistence of it.

Life doesn't pause for the sacred. It doesn't wait for rituals to finish or hearts to recalibrate. It doesn't mark absence with silence. It keeps operating on a schedule, oblivious to whether we're able to keep up.

She did what needed to be done. Showed up. Paid bills. Packed a suitcase. Grief didn't end her story. It just ran parallel to everything else. And the rest kept moving.

When I was maybe twelve, my family got a phone call that my oldest stepbrother had been killed in an accident at work. He was just eighteen, and it was his first job. I didn't know how to picture that. He wasn't someone I saw regularly, and the word "accident" felt too distant to carry the weight of what had happened. All I knew for sure is that I would not see him again.

Before that, my experience was quite different. I grew up around dogs. My mother bred and showed them, so from a young age, my sister and I were responsible for feeding, bathing, and helping care for the litters. It didn't feel unusual. We knew the routines. We knew which mothers were protective, which pups needed extra monitoring, and which dogs to steer clear of when they were injured or irritable.

Death was part of that rhythm. Newborns didn't always survive. Sometimes entire litters came early and didn't make it. Older dogs aged quickly, their bodies wearing down long before their personalities did. Some died from accidents, an open cabinet, a chewed bottle, or a medicine they couldn't metabolize.

Once, I accidentally dropped a dog. He wasn't heavy, and I wasn't careless. He wriggled at the wrong moment, fell from my arms, and landed on the concrete floor. His neck snapped. I stood over him for a long time, just staring. There was no blood. No noise. Just a silence that didn't feel empty, it felt final.

No one gave a speech. We wrapped him in a towel and buried him near the fence line with the others. There wasn't a ceremony. There was continuity. The other dogs still needed to be fed. Bowls refilled. Kennels cleaned. But I remember looking at his body and thinking, *So this is what happens. This is what it means to stop.* It was a body that once breathed, and then didn't.

I understood what it meant to stop. But I hadn't yet begun to wonder what happens next, or what it means that one day it would be me. It didn't begin when my grandmother died. That was over a decade ago, and I didn't think much about mortality then, not in any lasting way. Even when my mother passed, I moved through the motions. But about a year later, something shifted.

I was lying in bed, staring at the ceiling, thinking about the mess my sister and I had been left to sort through, papers, unanswered questions, all the decisions no one had prepared for. I didn't want to do that to my daughter. But what began as a practical concern turned into something else.

Where would I be when that time came? Not just what would happen to my things, but what would happen to me. Would I be asleep, as some scriptures suggest, those who sleep in the Lord will rise first? Or would I be in some kind of purgatory, as my father and his Catholic family believe, though that has never quite resonated with me?

Would I be aware of any passage of time at all? Or would it be the blink of an eye, one moment among the living, the next before the Throne of Glory? If time continues on without me, how long will I be remembered? And for what? A contribution? A presence? Or just for being missed, until I'm not?

That night, death stopped being theoretical. It became a threshold I would one day cross, and the question was no longer if, or even when, but what then?

No aging. No remembering. No becoming. Mom and grandma weren't somewhere else, doing something I couldn't see. They weren't waiting. They had exited sequence. That idea didn't comfort or devastate. It dismantled. Time stuttered. I studied the shadows on the ceiling with my eyes, unable to name what I felt. Only that time had changed shape.

We say someone is "no longer with us," meaning we can't see or touch them. But we rarely confront what it means that they are no longer temporal. They've left the structure that makes thought coherent, before, after, next, again. We don't often consider how disorienting that is.

The smallest interval we can measure with current atomic clocks is about one quintillionth of a second. In that frame, time doesn't feel like something you move through. It becomes granular, nearly particulate, stripped of all human texture. The cesium-133 standard, defining one second as over 9 billion oscillations of an atom's radiation state, is precise, repeatable, and entirely inaccessible to our felt experience.

At that scale, a moment is not a feeling or a perception. It's a cycle. A flick between quantum states. It has nothing to do with memory or presence. It doesn't wait for emotion to register. A star can age by a trillion of these units, and we'd barely grasp its passage.

Scientists have begun exploring even finer metrics, zeptoseconds and attoseconds, used to track electrons in motion. The shorter the interval, the more absurd the idea of a "now" becomes. Time, broken into slices too fine to inhabit. Not a flow, but a structure. And structures don't care if we understand them.

So when I say I remember a moment, I'm not referring to anything measurable. I'm claiming a feeling that physics doesn't recognize. My moment has no timestamp. But it held me, and I still haven't escaped it. The violence of that struck me. It wasn't the end of a life. It was the deletion of sequence. Narrative undone.

This is the question that persists: What actually disappears when someone dies?

The body, we bury. The memory we carry, but their location in time is gone. Their position in the current that still pulls us forward? Vanished.

Christian theology has wrestled with this. Paul's words in 2 Corinthians 5:8, absent from the body, present with the Lord, suggest immediacy. No interval. No waiting room. Yet the promise doesn't close the gap we feel. It doesn't resolve the existential rupture between someone's presence in our timeline and their absence from it.

Death isn't only the loss of the beloved. It's the collapse of rhythm. The reappearances. The pauses between calls. The spacing of presence. Erased from space, and from duration.

Even Christ's resurrection leaves the ache intact. He returns, wounds visible, but not to stay. His return is brief, transitional, threaded with mystery. Do not cling to me, he says to Mary. Why not? Because he is already beyond the story. Ascending not only to the father, but possibly beyond time.

There is a sacred cruelty here. The Psalms groan with it. Job dares to name it. "Man is like a breath," the Psalmist writes. "His days are like a fleeting shadow." But shadows require light. Breath requires presence. So what, then, is left when even those are gone?

What if the real question isn't what happens after we die, but what we think is happening now? If we trust the clocks, we live in measurable units. But our experience of time betrays those units constantly. We lose hours in grief. We stretch seconds in fear. We collapse decades into a memory.

So when someone dies, what vanishes might not be their body, or their mind, or even their voice. It might be their coordinates on our temporal map. Their presence held shape not only in space, but in rhythm. The time of their coffee. The intervals between their laughter. Their habits nested in our weeks. When they disappear, our sense of when collapses, too.

And if that's true, then death is not only an end, but a distortion. A ripple that bends the timeline we thought was stable. A person disappears, and with them, a whole sequence collapses.

So I ask again, not what happens when we die, but what disappears from time itself? The body, yes. The breath, yes. But also the calibration. The metronome. The invisible synchrony between selves. And if God holds time, then maybe the grief we feel is the soul's recoil from disintegration. From being asked to walk in rhythm alone.

The End of Story, or the End of Self?

There's a difference between fearing death and fearing disappearance. Most of us conflate the two. I wonder if what really unsettles us is the fear that when we go, the story goes too. The inner narration that made us feel like someone.

This fear is where science, despite its brilliance, begins to falter. Not in evidence. In experience. Neuroscience tells us that the self is an emergent construct formed by memory, brain patterning, and ongoing input. The "I" we identify with is less like a core and more like a chorus, a fragile synthesis that arises from neurons firing in synchrony, shaping continuity from raw signal.

When the brain dies, science suggests, so too does the illusion of a stable self. The internal narrator stops mid-sentence. The mind no longer assembles the next moment. No image to update. No new thread to tie to the past.

If the self is an illusion, why does its loss feel like annihilation?

Even Richard Dawkins once conceded that while we may be nothing more than "survival machines" for our genes, it still feels as if there's a self inside. And that feeling, that haunting coherence, demands more than reduction.

Christian theology does not reject the reality of the body. It also doesn't reduce the soul to the flicker of a synapse. It speaks of an essence breathed by God, a self known before the womb, remembered beyond the grave. In Isaiah, the voice of the Lord says: "See, I have engraved you on the palms of my hands." Not written. Engraved, etched into the eternal.

Still, there's mystery here. Even in Scripture, resurrection is not simply the continuation of life. It is transformation. The self is not erased. It is not preserved unchanged. Paul writes of a spiritual body, imperishable and different, yet somehow still you. This is not stasis. This is not a paused story waiting to resume. It is something entirely other.

Which brings me back to the fear. What if disintegration is what we dread? What if the real fear is being unmade?

In physics, entropy governs the universe: all things tend toward disorder. Left alone, systems decay. Order collapses. Information, unless preserved, becomes unrecoverable. In that light, death does not appear just as cessation. It appears as unraveling. The story breaks down. The voice stops speaking. The pages, once bound, scatter in the wind.

There are paradoxes here, too. At its edges, Quantum theory begins to suggest that information may not be truly lost, even in black holes. Hawking's own theory evolved to admit this possibility. What vanishes from view may not vanish from reality. And this, strangely, rhymes with theology.

The God who holds all things outside of time may also hold memory without decay. The one who calls the stars by name does not forget the whisper of a soul, even when the mind that formed it is dust. Perhaps the story ends. Maybe it ends in a book we don't yet know how to read.

Silence After the Symphony

There is something unnerving about the idea of no more. Not death as a veil, or journey, or sleep, but death as the full cessation of motion, sound, sequence. The symphony swells, crescendos, then cuts. Not to static. To silence. A silence without rest. Vacancy.

Theologically, we've long tried to soften this blow. We call death a passage, a return, a homecoming. We borrow metaphors of crossing rivers, climbing mountains, and ascending into light. We speak of banquets, reunions, and songs that do not end. And sometimes, when grief is raw, those images hold. They cradle us, lullabies for the soul.

What if nothing follows? What if there is no final verse? What if, after the music, there is only stillness?

This is where our spiritual frameworks begin to wrestle more honestly. The Hebrew Scriptures are, at times, conflicted about what lies beyond Sheol, the grave. Some passages suggest a shadowy persistence. Others imply total silence. "The dead do not praise the

Lord," Psalm 115 declares. And yet, Isaiah envisions a time when "your dead shall live; their bodies shall rise."

Myth, too, carries this ambivalence. In the Greek tradition, the afterlife is neither heaven nor hell, but a pale reflection, the asphodel fields, where souls wander like echoes. In the Egyptian Book of the Dead, elaborate rituals were needed just to secure the continuity of being. The Norse spoke of Hel as a place of forgetting. These mythologies are not naïve. They are poetic reckonings with absence.

Even these reckonings suggest something. Even in silence, they imagined a realm. A veil. A drifting. The idea of absolute nothingness, a void so clean it holds no echo, no watcher, no aftermath, is almost uniquely modern.

Perhaps that's why it haunts us.

The modern imagination, shaped by both science and secularism, often strips the mystery bare. It leaves the stage empty after the final act. Theology, at its best, does not rush to fill the silence. It sits with it. It mourns it. Then it listens.

In Revelation, John describes a moment in heaven when the Lamb opens the seventh seal. What follows is not glory or terror. It is silence. "There was silence in heaven for about half an hour." No trumpets. No thunder. Stillness.

What are we to make of that? Perhaps eternity, too, holds its breath. The end of time may not arrive in a blaze. It may come as a hush. A pause so absolute it becomes its own kind of presence.

This is not the comfort we usually seek. It may be the one we need. To learn not to fear silence. To recognize that the end of the symphony does not erase the Composer.

Perhaps what we call "nothing" is not absence. Perhaps it is a space too vast, too still, too sacred for our words to reach. A space where eternity does not follow time, but enfolds it.

I don't yet know what lies inside that pause. I doubt the answer lives in volume or certainty. Maybe that's why the next chapters turn not toward proof, but toward paradox. Toward the blink between this breath and the next. The quiet implosion of time. The crossing that cannot be marked.

Something is coming. Or nothing is. And we are already tuned in.

Chapter Two
What Is Null?

The Impossibility of Imagining Nothing

People like to say that grief reshapes you. It breaks you open and puts you back together wiser, deeper, truer. What if it didn't? What if it came and went like a low-pressure system, flattening everything in its path, then lifting, without transforming a thing?

For me, it wasn't a crucible. It was a hollowing.

The world lost its texture. I still moved, still worked, still answered texts. But the scaffolding underneath, the one I didn't know existed until it dropped, was gone. I wasn't transformed. I was emptied. Rebuilt never came. I just hung there, weightless.

Absence didn't shape me. It unshaped me.

And that's the trouble with nothingness. You can't grasp it. You can only feel the shape it used to fill, like air where a body once lay, like breath held too long, or a presence gone so completely it leaves no impression behind.

Try it. Close your eyes and picture nothing.

Darkness doesn't count. Darkness is something.

Silence doesn't count. Silence still has tone and tension.
Sleep won't do. Sleep is a hallway, an in-between.

Try again. Strip away color, then shape, then awareness of shape. Strip away sense, dimension, and location. Strip away time. Then strip away the you that is doing the stripping. What remains?

You won't get there. No one does. True null, the un-being of all being, is neurologically inaccessible. Unknowable. The mind, bound by evolution to model environments and preserve continuity, cannot conjure its own obliteration.

Neuroscientist David Eagleman once observed that "the brain's job is to model the world, and it does not model the absence of the modeler" (Eagleman, 2011). That sentence unsettled me more than any funeral sermon ever has. We can picture our bodies ceasing, even our memories thinning into static, but never the disappearance of the one doing the picturing. This isn't merely fear. It's a neurological impasse. Null doesn't live at the edges of consciousness. It lives beyond its architecture.

That makes it more terrifying than we admit.

We are, as a species, compulsively imaginative. We dream up alternate lives, distant planets, endless eternities. We build myth and religion to give contour to what would otherwise be blank. If null is real, if death is a total deletion of consciousness and time, we are not looking across a chasm. We are looking at a wall.

And the brain doesn't know how to look at a wall. It insists on a hallway.

Even atheistic or secular thinkers who assert a naturalistic model of death, "we return to the soil," "we blink out like a flame", use metaphors of transformation or conclusion. Absence without edge eludes linguistic grasp. Language was made for presence. Even silence has grammar.

Most cultures, when pressed, refuse complete nothingness.

The Greeks imagined Hades as a pale underworld where shadows roamed in forgetful half-being. The Buddhists conceived of nirvana, often mistranslated as annihilation, but more accurately rendered as unbinding. Illusion falls away, but something watches the falling. In the Christian mystic tradition, the cloud of unknowing is described as an obscured presence, a divine hiddenness so total it can only be felt as loss.

Even science, when confronting the question of nothing, gets tangled.

In physics, a vacuum is not empty. It's seething with quantum fluctuations, particles appearing and vanishing, space curving and stretching in response to invisible forces. What we call "nothing" is not the absence of everything. It's the potentiality of anything, a kind of womb.

Philosopher Martin Heidegger famously declared, "The nothing itself nothings." It was his way of naming the paradox: that we cannot think about nothing without making it into something. The instant we attempt to conceptualize non-being, we bring it into the sphere of being. This is why, he said, anxiety, not fear, is the purest confrontation with the void. Fear has an object. Anxiety doesn't. It is dread of a presence that never arrives or an absence that never leaves.

In modern secular culture, we like to dress up death in stoic acceptance. We say it's natural. We say it's just the end. Few sit with what "end" actually means. Transformation isn't part of it. Reunion isn't part of it. Just... cessation.

We turn away. Or we keep talking.

Maybe this is why silence makes us nervous. Its danger isn't in what it contains, but in how close it gets to nothing. And nothing, when fully faced, leaves no one behind to do the facing.

There is a psychological name for the state we try to simulate when we think about null: depersonalization. It's the eerie, dissociative sensation of watching yourself from outside yourself, like awareness has slipped the bounds of the body but can't quite vanish. But even this is a distortion of presence. It is too much of something in the wrong place.

If anything, our failure to imagine null may explain our obsessive need for afterlives, in religious doctrine, ghost stories, digital legacies, even quantum physics. We hedge against deletion with every story we tell and every data point we save. The unspoken fear is vanishing so thoroughly that there will be no echo.

Imagine a room where someone once lived. Not long ago.

The bed is still made. The coffee mug still sits on the counter, half-drunk. There's no sign of struggle, no noise, no mess. Just stillness. A strange, organized kind. Like the room is waiting.

You know, rationally, the person is gone. But something in you resists. This isn't grief. This isn't hope. Something quieter moves under it. The room feels too intact. Like if you breathe wrong, it might break the spell and reveal where they've gone.

Absence is louder when the setting stays the same. Because then it's not just that the person is gone. It's that they were just here. And now, there's no sound. No motion. No energy. Just an outline where once there was life.

This is what null feels like to the mind.

It's not blackness. It's a room with no one in it, where nothing has moved, and nothing will move again. A stillness so complete it becomes its own kind of noise.

I remember once, late at night, trying to picture what it would be like not to wake up. Not to die. To not be. It wasn't frightening exactly. It was worse. An ache. A static. My mind kept folding in on itself, like a screen buffering with no signal. I couldn't do it.

Instead, I imagined floating, or fading, or dreaming forever. My brain quietly replaced null with metaphor. It had to.

Science tells us the brain persists in activity even moments after clinical death, a final burst of coherence, some say. Perhaps a last attempt at meaning (Borjigin et al., 2013). What follows is uncharted. Unobservable. The maps we draw are made from within time, using the tools of a self still intact.

We are fish trying to model fire. So we do what we always do. We reach for symbols. For stories. For the possibility that what we cannot imagine might still be real.

Maybe there is no null. Maybe there's only the veil: a not-this, not-here, not-ever-again that still refuses to resolve into nothing.

And perhaps that's the mercy: that silence doesn't demand we disappear to perceive it. It only asks us to listen, even when we don't know who is listening back.

What Silence Reveals

There comes a point when language can go no further. Knowledge doesn't end there. It unravels. In that space, where answers collapse and presence can't be proven, we are left only with questions. These aren't tools. They're offerings. Flares cast into the dark, not to be answered, but to illuminate what haunts us in the quiet.

What if silence isn't empty?

What if what we call absence compresses presence, like a lung holding breath?

What if silence gives sound its shape?

What if space is where meaning lives between moments?

What happens to a story if no one remembers it?

What happens to a self if no one reflects it?

What if death unmirrors rather than deletes?

Can stillness be inhabited?
Can void be witnessed?
What do we hear in the pause after a final word?
What tension lives in the moment between heartbeat and no heartbeat?
Can nothing ache?
If time folds, does absence echo?
When we pray into silence, are we speaking into distance or into a presence too large to speak back?
Is there a difference?
What if the space we dread holds too much, not too little?
What if what we call void veils what comes first?
What if the silence doesn't mean we're alone, only that we've gone unheard?

Perhaps the questions themselves are the threshold. They don't gate meaning. They trace the contours of a silence too intelligent to speak. Maybe what waits beyond death, if anything does, is shaped less by what we believe and more by what we dare to ask. And maybe, just maybe, the void isn't answering because it already has. With stillness. With waiting. With the sound that only absence makes.

Faith in the Face of Null

Even the devout wake in the dark sometimes.

It's not always a crisis. It's not always doubt. Sometimes it's silence, the kind that follows fervent belief, like a breath held too long. One moment, faith is a cathedral lit from within. The next, it's an echo chamber. Still standing. Still sacred. Void of warmth.

What if there's nothing?

It's a question you're not supposed to ask out loud. Not in church pews. Not at deathbeds. And yet it visits the faithful like wind through a closed window, unseen, uninvited, undeniable. What if no one is waiting on the other side? What if the soul flickers and goes out? What if eternity erases everything?

The Apostle Paul writes, "If the dead are not raised, then our preaching is useless and so is your faith" (1 Corinthians 15:14). A startling admission. A theological high-stakes wager. Paul doesn't treat resurrection as metaphor or inspiration. He stakes the entire scaffolding of Christian hope on its fact. Without it, there is no defeat of death. And without that defeat, death remains what it feels like to us, a collapse.

Even Paul must have wrestled in the silences between letters. Jesus himself, in Gethsemane, pleads with God to let the cup pass. And from the cross: "My God, my God, why have you forsaken me?" (Matthew 27:46). These are not the cries of someone immune to the threat of nothingness. They are the words of a soul at the rim of absence.

Faith does not dissolve this terror. Sometimes it means looking straight at it and choosing hope anyway.

Across traditions, the possibility of null lingers like smoke behind the veil. In Egyptian funerary rites, the soul's survival was uncertain. One faced trials, spoke the forty-two negative confessions, and met the weighing of the heart. If the scales tipped wrong, if the heart outweighed the feather of Ma'at, the soul was devoured by Ammit. Final death. No afterworld. No return.

Buddhist traditions, though more cyclical, hold similar shadows. To fail to awaken leads back again and again into illusion. It isn't erasure in the Western sense, but the self never escapes, never sees, never reaches beyond impermanence. Liberation requires releasing even the self that fears vanishing.

Even our most transcendent myths don't fully banish the fear of nothing. They transfigure it.

For some, longing itself is evidence. "He has set eternity in the human heart," writes the Teacher in Ecclesiastes, "yet no one can fathom what God has done from beginning to end" (Ecclesiastes 3:11). The ache becomes a compass, pulling toward something, even if its shape stays veiled. Augustine called it restlessness: "Our hearts are restless until they find their rest in Thee." But what if that rest never comes? What if the ache is all we get?

It is a dangerous mercy that God does not answer every question.

There are moments, quiet and fragile, when the fear of null recedes. Belief doesn't harden. It loosens. You stop needing the future to be shaped like you. You stop needing survival to mean continuity. You begin to trust, not in what waits beyond death, but in the One you cannot imagine.

This is what the mystics hint at. Certainty fades. Surrender remains. A presence so full it no longer requires form.

To believe in the face of null isn't denial. It is reverence in full view of the void.

The Disappearing Witness

If a tree falls in the forest and no one hears it, does it make a sound?

The question is tired. The implication isn't.

If death is a true null, a full cessation of subjectivity, then the witness is gone. Erased. There is no one left to observe the falling tree, the forest, or the silence that follows. So the deeper question arises: if no one remains to observe reality, does reality remain?

Quantum physicists have long wrestled with this tension. In the double-slit experiment, light behaves differently depending on whether it is observed. When unmeasured, it behaves like a wave. When observed, like a particle. The implication, contested, often misunderstood, is that witnessing plays a role in outcome. That, in some strange and humbling way, the presence of an observer shapes reality.

But what happens when the observer is gone for good?

The question reaches beyond science. It cuts existentially. If I vanish, body, consciousness, awareness, what becomes of the world I once perceived? Do my children's faces still exist, or only for those who remain? Does the memory of my love persist, or does it dissolve when the last neuron that held it ceases to fire?

The ancient Greeks spoke of Lethe, the river of forgetting. Before reincarnation, the soul was said to drink and forget life. But the myth presupposes a drinker, a self who forgets. What if there is no drinker? No vessel left to carry even the forgetting? If null is complete, even memory's erasure cannot be witnessed. Forgetting itself dissolves.

We long to believe in a soul that outlives decay. However, much of what we call self is scaffolded by memory, time, and embeddedness in relationship. Strip these away, what's left? If null is deletion, the soul may disappear with the rest.

Some theologians counter with the doctrine of the imago Dei: that we are made in the image of God and eternally known, eternally held. Our preservation doesn't depend on self-memory. It rests in being remembered. God does not forget the witness. The self that disappears is, in divine terms, never lost.

Isaiah gives us this: "Can a woman forget her nursing child? ... Even these may forget, yet I will not forget you. See, I have engraved you on the palms of my hands" (Isaiah 49:15 - 16). The focus is not on our capacity to remember God. It is on God's refusal to un-know us, even in the grave.

But this assurance exists in tension with silence. From this side of the veil, the dead do not return to affirm their witness. We are left with a metaphysical asymmetry, a world observed by us, without verification that it is observed beyond us.

So we return to paradox.

If the soul persists without memory or time, is it still a witness? Or does it remain as presence stripped of perspective? If reality requires no observer, our vanishing means nothing. If it does, something unfathomable is lost each time a mind collapses into death.

One cannot solve this paradox. It resists resolution. It must be sat with, like grief, like awe, like a question too large for syntax.

Because in the end, the mystery is not whether anything remains when we are gone.

The mystery is that we were here to ask it.

Naming the Void

We name things to survive them.

That's one of the oldest truths of language, older than narrative, older than theology. Name the storm, and it becomes something you can track. Name the fear, and it has edges. Name the god, and you might persuade it to stay. But what happens when the thing we face isn't a thing at all, when it offers nothing to hold? What if naming it only creates the illusion that it exists?

We call it sleep. We call it night. We call it the end. None of these names hold.

Sleep implies waking. Night implies morning. An end implies it belonged to a story. Null, if it is real, has no shape. It cannot be pointed to. It cannot be recalled or anticipated. And still, we try. The alternative, to leave it unnamed, leaves us defenseless before it.

WHAT IS NULL?

In myth, even the gods were wary of nothingness.

In the Enuma Elish, before anything began, there was the mingling of Apsu and Tiamat, freshwater and saltwater, order and chaos. Creation comes from tension. Something inert, yes. Something undefined, never absent. In Hebrew scripture, the Spirit of God hovers over tohu va-bohu, formless and void. Chaos, not emptiness. And even that void gets named.

The Genesis account depicts God speaking into a soup of wildness. Light follows darkness. Form emerges through separation. Every created thing begins by being called. "Let there be..." is not only an act of creation. It is the start of naming. And through naming, restraint.

Even today, physicists speak of "nothing" with unease.

Vacuum states, quantum foam, zero-point energy, each one an attempt to define what lies beneath matter, beneath energy, beneath time itself. But none of them reach true null. They describe low states of activity. Substrate potentials. The backdrop to becoming. What they cannot touch is a state without observer, without frame, without equation.

So we cheat, without admitting it.

We name the void the way we name a god. Sometimes we call it peace. Sometimes we call it freedom. Sometimes we call it rest. These are euphemisms. They dress the abyss in linens and tuck it in. They soothe. They do not describe.

We say "passed away" instead of "ceased."

We say "laid to rest" instead of "disappeared."

We say "afterlife" even when we're unsure there was a before.

The language is soft for a reason. We're not ready to say what we mean.

When I was younger, I used to imagine death as a kind of drifting. Like letting go of a tether and slowly floating out past the edge of what can be seen. No pain. No destination. Just an infinite gray-blue dissolve.

It wasn't frightening, but it was still... something.

I realize now that it was never null that I was picturing. It was abstraction. Dream-state. A metaphor of death. Not death itself. To name it is to render it visible. To imagine it. And that is the great lie of the human mind: we think that what we name, we know.

The void resists naming.

It does not arrive dressed in black. It is not a sleep so deep it swallows morning. It is not a closing door, or a last breath, or a final frame in the reel. Those are transitions. Null has no direction, no motion, no before or after. Null erases the frame.

And yet.

There is something strange, almost sacred, about the names we give it anyway.

Perhaps naming is our form of prayer, a way of refusing to accept that something so total could go unlanguaged. Maybe the act of speaking into the dark honors it. The words are not meant to summon echo. They are meant to be said.

Even when they fall into silence.

Even when the silence does not fall back.

So we name the void.

We do it without defining.

Without controlling.

Only to mark that we stood near it.

That we, with our soft bodies and time-bound minds, came close enough to something we could not grasp, and still dared to speak.

Chapter Three

Time, Measured and Lost

Evening and Morning: Time as Servant, Not Sovereign

Time shifts shape depending on where you're standing inside it. As a child, a year looms like a mountain. As you age, it collapses into a shadow. I remember once standing at the edge of a lake in early spring, fog pressing against the water, the trees bare but trembling with the memory of green, and feeling, briefly, that I was outside of time. Nothing mystical happened. Everything simply stilled. The air held its breath, and so did I. There was no need to mark the moment. It was whole without a timestamp.

Stillness can soothe or unsettle. I once lost nearly a day without realizing it. It wasn't sleep or illness. Nothing collapsed or broke. A migraine began, then faded into a stretch of hours I couldn't recall. Dusk spilled across the blinds like ink. I had intended to rest for an hour. Instead, the world rearranged itself without me.

I didn't panic. I just sat up, disoriented by the tilt of the light. Something felt out of place, though I couldn't name it. My phone buzzed with messages. The to-do list I'd written in the morning sat untouched. I had been in the room the whole time, but detached from the structure that defines presence. It felt as if I'd slipped through a seam in the day and returned before it finished closing.

That evening, I moved slowly. I kept noticing how little of the day I could retrieve. No meals came to mind. No thoughts I could retrace. Just a gap. A blank space shaped like something that should have mattered. It didn't feel like restoration. It felt like absence. As if I'd ghosted my own life and left no trace.

That unsettled me more than exhaustion. I saw how deeply I depend on the continuity of time to locate myself. I string events together to maintain coherence, I did this, I felt that, I adjusted. I move through time, and it marks me. When sequence dissolves, I become unmoored. Present, but without placement.

Time doesn't just bracket experience. It shapes the sense of having lived it. Without it, meaning thins. Identity floats. And in that suspension creeps something close to grief, not for a person or a place, but for the loss of being somewhere and knowing you were.

I think now of those who live with that sensation every day. Those with dementia. Those in dissociative states. Those whose nervous systems loop through trauma without linear release. They don't just forget time. They lose the framework that helps the world stay named and navigable.

Perhaps this is why we cling to time so fiercely. Not to control it, but to remain visible within it. To be placed, located against the backdrop of motion. To be known as continuous.

That day lingers in memory precisely because nothing was recorded. I didn't check the time. I didn't note the hour to retell it later. The moment simply was, and then it wasn't. I wonder if that's a glimpse of how we were meant to live, embedded in a rhythm older than measurement.

Scripture opens not with a clock, but with cadence. "And there was evening, and there was morning, the first day" (Genesis 1:5). It confounds modern expectations. We assume the day begins with light. But in the sacred account, it begins in darkness. Evening first. Then morning. This isn't a poetic flourish; it's a liturgical pattern. The Hebrew day begins not at dawn or midnight, but at sundown. Time begins in rest.

That inversion carries theological weight. In the Genesis sequence, time does not govern creation. It serves it. Time flows within a world already breathing in cycles. Light and shadow. Work and Sabbath. Becoming and returning. Time is a structure meant to be entered, inhabited, then released.

Yet at some point in history, that sanctuary became scaffold. Time shifted from holding life to containing it. The calendar became sovereign. The hour, tyrant. The sacred rhythm broke. Time became a resource to be extracted, optimized, monetized, feared.

This shift carries consequences. If time once served divine order, what does it mean when time begins to rule it? When productivity defines worth. When grief has an expiration. When love is evaluated by its longevity instead of its depth.

Science tells its own story of time. It rarely speaks of holiness, yet it confirms ancient truths. Circadian biology shows that our bodies obey rhythms older than clocks. A cycle close to 24 hours is governed by the suprachiasmatic nucleus, a small cluster of neurons in the brain. Even in darkness, our biology leans toward repetition. We are tuned, at a cellular level, to the pulse of light and dark.

This suggests something profound. We don't merely observe time. We embody it. When trauma distorts that embodiment, through illness, aging, or psychic rupture, we don't just lose schedule. We lose cohesion. The architecture of memory falters. The story of the self stutters. We forget who we were. Who we loved. What mattered.

Time carries meaning. We narrate through it. A child's first step. A father's final breath. These aren't just events. They are coordinates. We become through them, marked by their placement in the sequence of our lives.

Imagine two sisters. One stays on Earth. The other boards a spacecraft. Not science fiction, but physics. According to Einstein's theory of special relativity, Alexa travels near the speed of light. Only a few years pass for her. Meanwhile, Cassie, her sister, waits on Earth. Decades unfold. Her hair grays. She raises children. She buries parents. She waits.

When Alexa returns, she is almost unchanged. Cassie is elderly. They embrace across an expanse that has no fixed measure. For Alexa, her sister's life accelerated. For Cassie, her sister disappeared into delay.

This paradox is real. Atomic clocks flown on jets have proven time's elasticity. The universe does not treat time as fixed. It tailors it to motion and gravity. Relativity fractures simultaneity.

And yet, theory does little to prepare us for the emotional dissonance.

In one imagined ending, Cassie dies just months after Alexa returns. Their reunion is brief. Alexa grieves what she missed, birthdays, arguments, the slow sediment of a shared life. She mourns a timeline she never lived. From her frame, Cassie aged too fast. From Cassie's, Alexa took too long.

The implication is sharp. Even love cannot guarantee shared time. Connection alone does not ensure overlap. If time can bend across galaxies, what happens at the border of death?

The question becomes intimate. If death is not an end, but an entrance into something timeless, how do we interpret the wait? Could one soul pass through and arrive instantly, while those behind stretch through years of longing? If eternity lacks sequence, is waiting even the right word?

The psalmist writes, "A thousand years in your sight are but as yesterday when it is past" (Psalm 90:4). God perceives time as gathered, not unfolding. Every ache, delay, or silence remains visible. Nothing is dismissed. Nothing disappears into the void.

Relativity may reveal the mechanics, but theology names the constancy. Time bends, but God does not. Love remains stable because it is anchored in a being not subject to sequence. Christian tradition has long insisted that time is not ultimate. "With the Lord a day is like a thousand years, and a thousand years are like a day" (2 Peter 3:8). This is not metaphor. It signals that eternity is not an infinite extension. It is a state beyond extension altogether. Presence without progression.

This distinction unsettles. If time dissolves, then memory as we know it might also change. Morality shaped by chronology might yield to something unfamiliar. What remains of us when the story stops unfolding?

Maybe that's why we keep our calendars. Why we light candles and observe anniversaries. They're not just habits. They're anchors. They hold us in a world that moves. To release time altogether feels like a kind of disintegration. Like standing again at the lake's edge, fog curling low, and agreeing to let the moment be holy without needing to name it.

Genesis does not ask us to command time. It calls us to remember where it began, in rhythm. In rest. Evening before morning. Descent before light. A pause before speech.

What would it mean to return to that rhythm? To see time not as a ladder to climb, but a breath rising and falling, given shape by something eternal?

Maybe the sacredness of time lies not in its passage, but in its posture. Bent toward the holy. Listening.

The Fear of the Untimed

There is a kind of quiet terror we rarely name, the fear of existing without time. No ticking clock. No next moment. No before or after. Just being without boundary. Or vanishing altogether.

Time gives shape to consciousness. It is not a backdrop, but the scaffold that allows awareness to cohere. To think is to move, forward in thought, backward in memory, outward in relation. Each motion relies on sequence. If time dissolves, what becomes of thought? What remains of the self?

Cognitive neuroscience offers clues, though they unsettle more than comfort. In temporal lobe epilepsy, near-death episodes, or prolonged sensory deprivation, people report deep distortions of time. Seconds stretch. Hours vanish. Events arrive all at once or scatter completely. The brain, unmoored from calibration, spirals. Some interpret these states as mystical. Many describe them as disorienting, even terrifying. The mind is not built for eternity. It is built for chronology.

Psychologically, the loss of temporal orientation erodes identity. Studies on Alzheimer's and advanced dementia confirm this. Patients lose more than memory. They lose continuity. Relationships collapse inward. Context disappears. The thread frays, and with it, the sense of being someone.

This fragility is not a flaw in evolution. It reflects our deepest design, continuity. We don't merely want to exist. We want to stretch across time, to see ourselves inside a story. Even grief, in all its violence, unfolds. It carries us through stages. It gives shape to loss. We lean on time to survive what time removes.

But if there is no time after death, if anything waits at all, what then? What happens to memory, to awareness, when sequence no longer applies? Can the self endure without before or after?

Tradition has offered many responses. Theology and myth resist finality. Eternity is often rendered as fullness, not extension. Christian mystics speak of a presence beyond time, where everything is reconciled. Meister Eckhart called it the "now-point," a stillness where the soul meets God, untethered from succession.

Even so, the imagination falters. Words strain. The Greek word aionios, often translated as "eternal," refers not to endless minutes but to quality shaped by divine presence. But how does one hold quality without duration? How do we step into a reality without past or future?

Myth has long created bridges to that unknown. The Egyptian Book of the Dead describes souls navigating symbols and trials. Tibetan Buddhism maps the bardo, a liminal space where time falters and projections rise. These traditions do not remove the terror. They recognize it. Disorientation is part of passage. Chronology must dissolve before the soul can find rest.

Perhaps this is a kind of mercy. To enter the infinite with finite cognition would break the mind. The brain is shaped for sequence, for effect that follows cause. It cannot stretch endlessly. If death gives anything, maybe it's this: the frame shatters, and what held us makes room for something larger to receive what remains.

For now, we remain within time. We set alarms. Light candles. Mark anniversaries. Even devotion unfolds sequentially, prayer, fasting, pilgrimage. These are not simply practices. They keep us tethered. They keep us from slipping away.

So the fear persists, not only fear of death, but of losing time's coherence. Of drifting beyond the reach of what comes next.

Yet within that fear, something quieter: if time is only a garment consciousness wears, its removal may not mean loss. It may mean transformation.

We look for ways to remain oriented. Simple actions, stretching bread dough, tracing shadows on the floor, stepping outside to hear wind in the branches, become provisional rituals. Not formal liturgy, but acts of return. They bring us back to motion shaped by gravity, not data. A pace slow enough for awareness to enter.

The need is not just spiritual. It is physiological. The body asks for rhythm. The nervous system settles only when patterns emerge, light fading, breath deepening, sound repeating. In trauma studies, this is called entrainment. It's how infants regulate. How monks center. How the world once signaled time before screens outshouted the sky.

We crave not just duration, but distinction, something that breaks the blur. A practice that says: now begins. Now ends. Something tactile enough to reattach us to the present. A bell rung at dusk. A warm bowl carried to the table. A pause before speech. These gestures do not restore sequence fully. But they suggest it. They let the body know that not all motion is endless.

And in their quiet offering, they answer the fear of disintegration with a gentler question: what if coherence can begin again? The return may not come through memory or schedule. It begins with attention. With the simple act of noticing what holds.

We rejoin time not by force, but by touch. Perhaps the sacred is not only held in the grand rites, but in the subtle tethering acts that say, we are still here, still moving, still becoming, even when we cannot yet name where we are in the story.

I've felt that ambiguity in both sanctuary and kitchen. I've sat through Good Friday vigils where time thickened with sorrow, each minute echoing deeper than the one before. I've stood at my counter at dusk, light shifting just enough to erase everything, no thought, no name, only a presence that pressed close.

I don't name those moments mystical. But they registered more sharply than the hour could explain. It didn't extend. It held. Time didn't vanish, it became still enough to feel.

Maybe that is eternity, presence so complete it doesn't require length. Fullness that arrives without unfolding.

We need both: the rhythm that steadies and the silence that releases. Sacred time gathers us. Sacred absence lets us be gathered.

The soul, it seems, needs both scaffold and sky.

Sacred Time vs. Sacred Absence

There is a holiness in keeping time. Lighting candles on Fridays. Kneeling at set hours. Marking seasons by the story of salvation. Advent. Lent. Ordinary Time. These rhythms hold space not only for God, but for us, to return, to remember, to step back into a story greater than our own.

Liturgical time is more than a calendar. It creates belonging. We reenter birth, death, and resurrection not as memory, but as invitation. Repetition does not diminish meaning. It builds it. The same story, faithfully reinhabited, begins to reshape us.

This rhythm echoes the ancient Hebrew imagination, where time spirals instead of advancing in a line. Passover becomes both event and mirror. Sabbath becomes both rest and awareness. These patterns describe a God who is not distant in eternity but present inside sanctified time. It matters that Jesus entered time. He was born into chronology. He aged. He grieved. The Incarnation affirms Genesis: time, rightly held, is not confinement. It carries the sacred.

The mystics speak of another form of holiness, beyond recurrence. They name a presence so complete it borders on absence. A God so near that the lines between moments and between selves blur.

Julian of Norwich, caught in vision, described not hours but a point where everything is held. Teresa of Ávila emerged from prayer unable to say what she had seen or how long she had been gone. These aren't analogies. They are accounts of a reality that touches this one.

Traditions converge around this experience. In Zen, satori dissolves the structure of time instantly. In Sufi longing, union is not ahead but already present. Even Revelation does not end with duration, it closes with a city lit from within, where "there is no more night" (Revelation 22:5). Not infinite day, but presence that does not end.

This is not contradiction. Sacred time and sacred absence belong together. The Church calendar holds us in repetition. The mystic vision strips that scaffolding. One calls us to presence. The other, to release.

I have lived both. I have sat in Good Friday services where sorrow slowed the room to a hush. I have stood in my kitchen at dusk, light falling in a way that erased everything, no words, no self, only a still ache that felt like God.

I can't verify what it was. I don't name it mystical. But it felt truer than the clock. It didn't stretch. It didn't have to. It was whole.

Maybe that is eternity, not a span, but a saturation. Not extension, but arrival.

We need both: the rhythm that roots us and the silence that alters us. Sacred time helps us remember who we are. Sacred absence reveals who God is.

The soul, it seems, needs both structure and sky.

Fractured Rhythms, Sacred Returns

There is a kind of time we now inhabit that feels suspended, digitally flattened, unanchored from physical cues. You can spend hours scrolling, typing, reacting, emotionally engaged, yet untouched by place. The room remains unchanged. The body stays seated. But the mind races in every direction, consuming and performing while the present dissolves.

This is not just distraction. It is disembodiment.

Digital time does not rise or fall. It has no dusk, no dawn. Unlike hunger or fatigue or the arc of sunlight, it does not signal itself. It simply continues. Perpetual refresh. The algorithms behind our screens do not respond to season or Sabbath. They operate outside the pulse of created rhythm. Feed. Loop. Click. Scroll.

The result is an illusion of infinite now. Always in time for the next post. The next message. The next alarm. But this "now" has no edge. No boundary. It is not shaped by presence. It offers no weight. It exists as a unit in a stream without sequence. There is no evening and morning here. No day to mark from another.

This shift is not only cultural. It is neurological. Studies in media use show how sustained screen activity dampens interoception, the brain's ability to register internal bodily states. Hunger softens. Posture stiffens. You forget how long you've been sitting. The body, once the keeper of lived time, grows quiet.

And when the body stops marking time, the soul begins to feel its absence.

We may not notice what's gone until we try to reenter time that moves. To walk outdoors. To feel the wind. To watch light shift across walls. To remember ourselves not as devices, but as beings shaped by breath and gravity.

In some ways, digital time resembles what we fear about death, awareness without anchor. Perception without location. Activity without embodiment. But unlike death, this is permitted. And unlike sacred timelessness, it yields no fullness. Only depletion.

Perhaps this is why sacred traditions hold fast to rhythm. To liturgy. To embodied acts. Candles lit at nightfall. Bread torn by hand. These are not empty repetitions. They ground us. Without them, we are not released from time, we are displaced by it.

We keep time because we fear its disappearance. Not only through clocks, but through ritual. Calendars. Gestures. The instinct predates measurement. Before sundials or feasts, there were fireside stories, blood on doorposts, stones placed in memory.

To be human is not only to move through time, but to need markers inside it. Symbols that say: this mattered. This was real.

And still, a paradox. The more sacred the event, the more ritual tries to transcend what it marks. Take the Eucharist. "Do this in remembrance of me." A command to commemorate, yet the act enacts presence. It does not retell a death. It enters it. Not history, but participation.

Or consider a candle lit for a child who died. It returns each year. The child does not age. Time advances. But the ritual repeats. Not to undo time, but to testify, time did not erase this.

Even secular rhythms reach toward the sacred. The New Year's countdown is not about arriving. It names the threshold. It holds the breath between what has ended and what has begun.

Liturgical seasons do this with care. Advent. Lent. Pentecost. Each carries a memory already given. But in the retelling, it becomes present again. Repetition does not wear meaning thin. It protects it. It makes it touchable.

And still, each ritual contains its own vanishing. The candle fades. The bread is consumed. The body returns to earth. What remains is not the act itself, but the moment it tried to hold.

Here, the mystics and the mourners find one another. They know ritual does not preserve time. It honors it. It says: we remember because we are finite. We light candles not to stop eternity, but to mark where we once stood before it.

Perhaps this is mercy. That in marking time, we point beyond it. That in the flicker and the silence, in the cycle and the return, we meet the God who both enters and transcends all time.

Not in span.

In recognition.

Chapter Four

THE ETERNAL BLINK

"Absent... Present" and the Dissonance of Instantaneity

There is a phrase many Christians know by heart, though few pause to feel its strangeness: "To be absent from the body is to be present with the Lord." A promise drawn from Paul's second letter to the Corinthians (2 Corinthians 5:8), it is often recited at funerals with doctrinal ease, a comfort offered without pause. But if we hold the words in the light of actual dying, the real, aching moment when a body slackens and someone we love ceases to respond, they do not resolve the mystery. They intensify it.

It's not just a promise; it's a paradox.

Absent... present. The ellipsis is mine, but perhaps it always belonged there. For what does it mean to vanish from time and appear in eternity in the same instant? No passage. No waiting. No in-between. Just a divine conjunction, as though God could fold reality like paper, pressing two distant points together.

Yet the original Greek is not quite so immediate. The phrase often translated as "to be absent from the body and present with the Lord" is more cautiously rendered in context: "We would rather be away from the body and at home with the Lord" (2 Corinthians 5:8). The verb ἐνδημέω (endēmeō) implies dwelling, habitation, something more rooted than arrival. It suggests that presence with God involves belonging. Meanwhile, the "absence" from the body (ἐκδημέω, ekdēmeō) carries the sense of being away from home, like a traveler in exile.

Paul is not drawing a clean line from heartbeat to heaven. He is navigating tension, existential as much as theological. One that does not erase the blink. It sanctifies it.

And still, the question remains: how can presence occur without passage? How can eternity take hold in an instant?

A blink is the briefest erasure we permit ourselves. It lasts a tenth of a second, enough to moisten the eye, reset focus, restore vision. We blink twelve to twenty times a minute, and never once does the world disappear. Our minds fill the gap, weaving continuity over the microsecond break. A blink is not an absence. It is a protected lapse. One we never notice.

But death is not that kind of blink. It does not restore focus. It ruptures it.

We call death a blink to soften the blow. But what actually happens between the last inhale and whatever follows, if anything, is not a blink in any physiological sense. It's a chasm mistaken for a dash. A moment so profound we dare not look at it without metaphor.

To call it "just a blink" is to assume continuity. But continuity is precisely what we lose.

What if it is not the blink of the eye, but the blink of a star, flaring into collapse, light reaching us long after the source is gone?

The physical blink protects the eye from dryness. The eternal blink exposes the soul to what cannot be seen.

One is a rhythm. The other, a rupture.

We cannot grasp the instant when the soul, if soul there is, slips its housing. We only sense the after: the silence, the stillness, the uncanny vacancy. And if the transition is instantaneous, it is not gentle.

It is disorienting. Not because it happens so fast, but because it happens outside time altogether.

The dissonance deepens when we consult the mind's own architecture. From a neurological perspective, perception is never truly immediate. The act of seeing is delayed, light strikes the retina, signals are relayed, patterns are reconstructed. Every moment we think we're living in has already passed. The brain is always catching up, assembling the world just behind its unfolding.

When death arrives, it reaches a brain already behind. And if there is a final moment of awareness, it moves through delay. A presence that comes "immediately" still passes through a perceptual gap.

Physics offers no reprieve. According to Einstein's theory of relativity, simultaneity depends on perspective. What occurs "at once" in one frame may unfold at different times in another. There is no universal now, only reference points.

So when we imagine the soul departing to meet God in a flash, what clock are we using? The faltering heartbeat? The cellular unraveling that continues? The final neural surge? Or the calendarless time of eternity, where nothing passes because nothing is measured?

Paul doesn't treat eternity like a destination we'll reach once we've finished dying. He speaks instead from the ache of waiting. "For in this tent we groan, longing to be clothed with our heavenly dwelling" (2 Corinthians 5:2). That groaning isn't despair. It's the soul's response to a presence we can sense but not hold.

The blink resists interpretation not because it's empty, but because it's full beyond our measure. Whatever waits on the other side isn't taken. It's given.

Maybe theology's task isn't to resolve the paradox at all, but to stand beside it and call it holy.

To see the blink as a liminal space, however unmeasurable, does not shrink the promise. It enlarges it. The more we allow for dissonance, the less likely we are to confuse silence with absence.

Eternity does not need to explain itself. But we, creatures of rhythm and narrative, reach for metaphors that strain to hold it. Sometimes, the most honest act is to pause mid-sentence, absent... present, and leave the silence intact.

I once heard a hospice nurse describe the moment a patient passed, and I've never forgotten her words. "He was speaking to his daughter," she said. "They'd been talking about something ordinary, grocery lists or laundry, I think. Then he blinked, as if pausing to remember something, and that was it. He never opened his eyes again." There was no dramatic final breath, no whisper of farewell. Just an inhale, and then... stillness. The daughter hadn't even realized what had happened until a few seconds passed and he didn't respond. "Dad?" she asked, touching his arm.

In my own family, my mother-in-law told me of her experience when her husband passed away. They were watching tv one afternoon, as they did at times. He closed his eyes to drift off as to nap. She called over to him to come to dinner a short while later, and he didn't answer. He was still sitting back in his recliner, dozing. When he didn't rouse when she tried to wake him, that's when she realized he was gone.

The women in both instances emphasized the ordinariness of it. Again there was no sign. Nothing to indicate anything other than the ordinary had happened. Neither realized their loved one was no longer among the living.

Gone.

What haunts me most about these personal accounts is their suddenness. "He was there," they said, "and then he wasn't. No in-between. Just gone. Like someone exiting a room too quietly to notice."

I've thought of that often. Not because it's unusual, but because it isn't. The mind craves thresholds. We want bells, warnings, signposts. But death often moves more like a shadow leaving a surface, quiet, unnoticed, like "a thief in the night" (1 Thessalonians 5:2) Scripture warns will come when no one is watching. One moment, shape and presence. The next, only light.

A blink. A breath. And the world keeps turning.

The Blink as Threshold or Trick of Perception?

The notion of "the blink" is deceptively gentle. It evokes a moment so swift we barely register its passing. A closing and opening of the eyes. A pause so brief it seems to vanish in its own occurrence. Yet applied to death, the image turns paradoxical. Something disappears entirely. And if the promises of many faiths hold, something also begins.

But how can eternity occur within the space of a blink? Or is that very span a false frame?

Science, when honest, does not follow us beyond death. But it has much to say about what happens just before. The brain does not go dark all at once. Research shows a surge of neural activity, sometimes even heightened gamma waves, linked in life to consciousness, perception, and sensory integration (Borjigin et al., 2013). One study described this as a kind of neurological crescendo. The dying brain lights up briefly, as if reaching for something even as the body lets go.

Could this blink be more than silence? Could it be a burst of perception, a moment stretched from the inside, more expansive than it appears from without?

This does not claim the soul confirms its release in those final waves. It does suggest that what seems instantaneous to an observer may feel otherwise within the mind. If perception shapes time, and all evidence suggests it does, then death may feel less like a blink and more like a crossing. A widening. An unfolding.

Einstein's theory of general relativity deepens the mystery. Time slows in the presence of gravity. Near a black hole, it dilates so severely that what lasts seconds for one observer might span centuries for another. If consciousness endures briefly beyond the body, the mind might perceive time stretching beyond the clock's final report. The blink could hold multitudes.

Yet this remains conjecture. No equation accounts for the soul. No experiment has traced the final threshold and returned with certainty. The closest we come is metaphor.

Myths have always spoken the language of thresholds. In Greek tradition, Hermes escorts souls to the underworld, his winged sandals skimming the border between realms. In Egyptian belief, Anubis weighs the heart before passage. In Tibetan Buddhism, the bardo is a liminal space, a transition between death and rebirth. These images acknowledge what science cannot: that transition may itself be terrain.

If so, the blink is not absence. It is a landscape without measure. A suspension of time. A space where categories collapse, before, after, here, gone.

The mind resists this. We are creatures of sequence. We want the blink to be one thing. A moment. A metaphor. But perhaps it is both. A neurological event and a symbol for what lies beyond understanding.

The danger lies in chasing clarity where none belongs. If the blink is a threshold, we do not need to name what it leads into. If it is a perceptual trick, that does not strip it of reverence. Either way, it marks a mystery, the unmaking of the time-bound self.

Whether death feels instantaneous or infinite may depend less on what occurs, and more on what it means to leave time at all.

Across the great sweep of spiritual traditions, one motif persists: the crossing happens fast.

Not always in story, but in symbol. The lightning bolt. The breaking dawn. The chariot of fire. The soul, when it leaves, does not crawl. It flashes. It vanishes. It is caught up, carried away, torn through space and veil. Time does not stretch to contain it. Time, if anything, is bypassed.

In the Hebrew scriptures, Elijah is taken suddenly by "a chariot of fire and horses of fire" (2 Kings 2:11). There is no preparation. One moment, he walks beside Elisha. The next, he is gone, caught up in a whirlwind, not laid gently into the ground. It is not a slow death. It is a rupture.

In the New Testament, Jesus' transfiguration is described in sudden, searing brightness. "His face shone like the sun," Matthew writes, "and his clothes became dazzling white" (Matthew 17:2, Luke 9:29). There is no slow fade. No soft glow. Just sudden radiance. Unbearable. Unmistakable. The disciples fall to the ground. Glory does not unfold, it breaks in.

The Tibetan bardo experience is said to unfold in rapid transitions. One moment, the soul sees brilliant light; the next, it may recoil, turning toward more familiar illusions. The teachings emphasize swiftness, flashes of clarity, fleeting chances for liberation, all passing in quick succession. The soul does not drift gently. It is thrust into a realm where perception speeds beyond recognition.

Even the Qur'an describes the final moment as swifter than we can imagine: "The matter of the Hour is not but as a twinkling of the eye or even nearer" (Qur'an 16:77).

These images don't agree on what happens after, but they agree on this: it happens fast. So fast it defies witnessing.

The transition from time into eternity is never portrayed as gentle descent. It is rupture. Fire. Light. Thunder. Disappearance.

And maybe that's because any transition from the temporal into the eternal cannot be gradual. The soul cannot acclimate to eternity the way one adjusts to a darkened room.

It must be pierced by it.

Living Inside a Vanishing Point

There is a moment in grief no one prepares you for. It is not the funeral. Not the empty house. It comes later, often without announcement, when the finality settles not as shock but as borderless absence. You realize, with an ache beyond words, that the person hasn't left in any directional sense. They have vanished.

And that vanishing, the sudden absence without passage, confronts us not only with death, but with the structure of eternity itself, something unthinkable, outside sequence.

We live our lives inside story. Even without grand narratives, we build meaning through sequence: this led to that; he became; she changed; I learned. Time shapes the soul. But the blink, the vanishing point between life and eternity, refuses story. It collapses the arc. A door closes. No sound. No visible motion. One moment, breath. The next, stillness. No frame to soften the shift.

This is why myth matters. Myths don't explain. They hold. They offer image where explanation breaks. The blink, mythically seen, is not a moment. It is a symbol of beyondness. A punctuation that breaks open.

The Celts spoke of thin places, geographic or spiritual spaces where the veil wears thin, where presence and absence flicker like candlelight. The blink may be the thinnest place of all. Not a location. A collapsing of dimensions. A crossing without movement. A farewell without distance.

Theologically, this is both unbearable and beautiful. The Christian imagination struggles to depict eternity without time, presence without sequence. We speak of resurrection, reunion, divine embrace. But these metaphors lean on constructs like then, again, forever. The change, if it comes, may not unfold at all. It may arrive in stillness. In the unraveling of sequence itself.

To live with this paradox is not to resolve it. It is to be shaped by it.

If death is a passage, it's not filmed like a slow fade. It's a hard cut.

Cinema, perhaps more than theology, knows how to signal finality. A door slams. A screen goes black. A character vanishes between frames. The jump cut, a sudden transition from one shot to another without warning, mimics how loss often feels in real life. Jarring. Discontinuous. Real but unreal.

One moment, you are watching someone tie their shoes. The next, you are at their funeral. No in-between. The audience has to catch up, fill in what's missing. There was a story. Now there is a hole.

Time in film is elastic. Directors compress, stretch, or erase it to shape emotion. But death, true, unfilmable death, resists portrayal. And so, when it's represented, it often arrives as rupture. Think of the sudden silence after a gunshot. The light that flares, then cuts to black. The absence that replaces presence so quickly the mind stutters to keep pace.

This mirrors what many experience in grief. We expect a process. We get a discontinuity.

The hard cut isn't just a cinematic trick. It's a perceptual truth. Cognitive science tells us that the mind makes sense of continuity by stitching frames together. When too much changes between frames, too much light, too much movement, the illusion breaks. We feel the cut. We flinch.

And yet, the cut is real. The blink, the death, the loss, these aren't transitions the mind can narrate cleanly. They resist sequencing. Like the soul skipping a beat and landing in a different key.

If we're honest, most of what we imagine about death borrows from editing. The fade-out. The dissolve. The upward pan into clouds.

But maybe what's truer is the smash cut. One shot. Then gone.

Not to diminish the sacred. But to acknowledge the rupture.

The blink isn't a cinematic flourish. It's a raw discontinuity.

We don't cross the threshold gradually.

We are taken there.

I remember sitting beside my grandmother as she neared the end. In those final days, her body was clearly shutting down, but I was still trying to reverse it, calling her doctors, managing medications, doing whatever I could to keep her here just a little longer. It took time for me to understand that it was her time to go.

When I did, I sat by her side, her hand in mine, and did the only thing I could think to do. I prayed the sinner's prayer aloud, and then I began to speak the words of Jesus: In my Father's house are many mansions. I go to prepare a place for you, so that where I am, you may be also.

My voice grew louder as I spoke, until I was nearly shouting. And when the words stopped, I looked down. She was still. Then she took one long, final breath, and she was gone.

I sat there for what felt like minutes. I knew she was gone, but my mind couldn't wrap itself around what had just happened. She wasn't there. Her body was just that now, a body. An empty garment.

I thought of all the scenes from movies and television where people sob beside the dying, cradling them, kissing their faces. But that didn't make sense to me. She wasn't in that body anymore. Whatever had animated her, whatever I had loved, she had taken it with her.

That feeling never left. Grief came too, but what stayed was awe. A destabilizing sense that death is more than loss. It is a mystery that reshapes the living.

What does it mean to be present for your own vanishing?

Not as metaphor. Not from the witness's side. But from within. At the seam between breath and no breath. Between heartbeat and hush.

We know what the body looks like from the outside as it dies. Muscles slacken. Hands grow cool. The chest stills. But inside, in that unlit interior where awareness has always lived, what stirs then? Does the self feel its own uncoupling? Or is the final moment mercifully veiled?

Maybe the soul isn't yanked from the body, but loosened. Unfastened like thread pulled gently from cloth. Maybe there's a moment when the self is still in the body, but no longer of it.

Does the body know? Not consciously. But perhaps at some level, beyond language, the body registers the invitation. The descent. The drift. A final yielding, not to absence, but to something that does not require continuation.

And what of the soul? If it remains aware, if awareness itself remains, does it resist or recognize what's happening? Is there fear? Wonder? Surrender?

Some traditions say the soul is summoned. Others say it is released. Still others say it is received. Each word implies a different kind of presence. A different kind of being felt as one slips.

What if the last moment is not an ending, but an arrival so immediate we mistake it for disappearance?

From this side, death appears as silence. But from within, it may feel like the first note of something vast. The moment the tether goes slack, not as failure, but as completion.

If the soul is present in that moment, even briefly, then it is not watching from a distance. It is crossing. It is leaving not because it must, but because it is being called.

And the body, reverent to the end, lets it go.

To grieve in light of the blink is to walk near something unspeakably holy. It teaches reverence, not only for the one gone, but for the space they passed through. A space we too will enter. The blink does not offer comfort. It invites humility. It says: this is not yours to see. Not yet.

And yet it shapes everything.

The blink is not the end of story. It is the end of sequence. The soul may continue, though not in chapters. Love may endure, though not in years. Meaning may deepen, though not along a timeline. The blink is not only a vanishing. It is a reorientation. A stripping away of narrative scaffolding. A mythic signal that the truest things may defy articulation.

We do not live at the edge of eternity. We live inside the tension it creates.

And if we listen, the silence the blink leaves behind is not void. It is echo.

Reflection: The Light Between Lids

Try this:

Close your eyes, not in fear, not in sleep, but in stillness.

Notice the space behind them. The dim warmth. The light that lingers even after the world goes dark.

That is not absence. It is the trace of something just beyond perception. A brightness without image. A nearness without touch.

Maybe the blink is not what ends our seeing.

Maybe it's what begins our becoming.

PART II: THROUGH THE VOID

CROSSING OVER WITHOUT EVER KNOWING WE DID

Chapter Five
The Void as Threshold

Death and the Symbol of the River

There is a reason so many cultures imagine a river at the edge of death.

The Greeks called it Styx, a dark, stilled boundary across which souls were ferried by a silent oarsman who never turned his face. In Egyptian myth, the soul navigates the subterranean Nile of the Duat, flanked by guardians, prayers, and perils. In Norse tradition, the Gjöll river flows beneath a bridge where the dead are judged as they pass. And in the Christian imagination, though less explicitly, a watery edge lingers. The Jordan, for instance, became more than a geographic boundary. It is a sacred threshold sung in old spirituals and funeral sermons: "I won't have to cross Jordan alone."

These rivers frame a passage. Each one marks a point of transit between realms.

And crossings imply there is something on the other side.

It may be no accident that water resists permanence. A river always moves, even when it appears still. It carries things away and delivers things forward. It carves canyons, gathers silt, remembers floods. The mythic soul, like the water beneath it, is not asked to remain, but to yield to motion.

Yet for the living, the idea of being carried where we cannot go ourselves feels like a kind of violence. We anchor meaning in choice and direction. The final passage may ask for neither. In myth, the river does not wait. The boatman does not pause. The traveler does not return.

In biblical theology, death is not often shown as a literal river, but the metaphor persists. Psalm 23 speaks of the "valley of the shadow," a dim threshold with no map, only a rod and a staff. In Luke 16, Jesus tells of a "great chasm" fixed between the living and the dead, a void even the longing gaze of the rich man cannot cross (Luke 16:26). And yet, the prophets speak of God making "a way in the sea, a path in the mighty waters" (Isaiah 43:16), suggesting that the One who parts rivers may also walk with us through them.

In this framing, the void is a veil. What is hidden may still be inhabited. We fear the water not because it is empty, but because we cannot see what stirs beneath its surface.

The earliest Christian funerals echoed this theme of sacred passage. The body was not discarded, but prepared, washed, wrapped, and laid as if for a journey. The rituals did not seek to delay the inevitable. They sought to honor it, to mark that something irreversible was unfolding, something solemn and holy. As early as the 2nd century, the apologist Minucius Felix described death as "a journey to a better place," borrowing from Stoic and Egyptian echoes alike.

What unites these river images is reverence for in-betweenness. The boat is neither origin nor destination. The boat holds that middle space, suspended between departure and arrival.

And perhaps that is what the myth was always trying to say.

A river makes no claim to permanence, but it marks what matters. Even in dry seasons, the shape it carved remains. We speak of liminal spaces as though they are vague or transitional, but the mythic river is precise. It defines the limits of flesh, intention, and memory. The boat does not meander. It follows a current set by something older than human will.

In Rabbinic literature, water often signals chaos and creative power. Before light, before speech, the Spirit of God hovered over the deep. Chaos was not banished; it was contained. The Hebrew word *tehom*, the deep, is not a villain. It is the womb of creation. To cross the waters, then, is not to escape the world, but to return to the place where the world began.

The soul's crossing, imagined in so many forms, does not follow the logic of ascent. It is a descent into mystery. The Orphic initiates in ancient Greece carried gold leaves inscribed with instructions for the underworld: reminders of who they were and where they belonged. Early Christians, too, left symbols, fish, anchors, doves, on tombs, not as decoration but as a form of resistance. Against death's silence, they marked the passage as known, even if not spoken.

In this light, faith is not certainty about what lies beyond. It is reverence for the crossing itself. The boatman may have no name. The river may offer no map. But to prepare the body, to sing at the banks, to whisper prayers into the hush, these are acts of orientation. They do not demand the return of the departed. They do not bargain with absence. They testify that even in threshold spaces, there is order, however hidden. There is purpose, even in the drift.

And if the river is a veil, it is not drawn by human hands. It parts only when it must. Until then, we tend its banks with memory and myth, shaping what we can of the unseen.

Archetypes of Passage

Across centuries, the dead have rarely been imagined as still. They move. They travel. They cross through something. We may not know what lies beyond, but the body seems to carry a memory of motion.

Ancient Egyptians envisioned the Duat as a layered passage, a sequence of gates, guardians, and reckonings. In Tibetan Buddhism, the Bardo appears as a field of visions, shaped by attachment and the soul's readiness to release. In hospice rooms, patients often describe travel preparations, waiting for someone, gathering things, sensing a door that's about to open.

These aren't data points. They're echoes. They remind us that dying has always been imagined as a crossing. Less an end than a movement. Less erasure than encounter.

Why does this motif endure, in spiritual visions and clinical observations alike? Because when pressed to imagine the end, the human mind does not default to stillness. It dreams of motion. Of through.

Theologically, Scripture affirms this movement. Jesus tells the thief on the cross, "Today you will be with me in paradise." Paul echoes this in 2 Corinthians: believers are "away from the body" and "at home with the Lord." These are not static states. They describe transition. The language assumes a crossing.

Even in Genesis, with the first death, Abel's, the framing resists annihilation. When God confronts Cain, He says, "The voice of your brother's blood is crying to me from the ground." Abel is no longer alive, yet something of him still speaks. That cry carries motion. Witness. Presence.

Science, though cautious, also leaves space open. Some physicists suggest that time may not be linear at the most fundamental level. Carlo Rovelli has argued that time might emerge from thermodynamic and relational processes, rather than exist as a fixed backdrop. If so, death may not mark an end. It could signal reconfiguration.

This does not mean the dead move through a literal hallway or rise through layers. It means the language of passage may not be mere metaphor. It may be the closest articulation we have for something deeper than duration and more active than cessation.

In all these visions, mythic, theological, clinical, and theoretical, death is not a wall. It opens like a corridor, and we move through it with a knowledge older than speech.

Motion alone does not sanctify the passage. What makes it meaningful is the direction it awakens in us. The crossing is not merely from life to death, but from known to unknown, from formed identity to something unshaped and unseen. That transition draws out not only fear, but also a fierce kind of memory, an intuition of having passed through before.

In Jewish mysticism, the soul is said to traverse stages both before birth and after death. The Zohar speaks of a river of light that souls must cross on their way to rejoin the source from which they came. In this framework, the end is not a destination. It is a return through veils that once clothed the spirit in flesh.

Christian mystics, too, sensed this return. Julian of Norwich described death as "beholding God," not as an encounter with judgment alone, but with the truth of one's own being in the light of divine mercy. For her, the transition was not negation. It was clarity. A stripping away of all that occludes love.

This sense of movement toward essence, rather than away from life, offers a counterweight to modern obsessions with biological finality. The soul's momentum, in these visions, is not spent. It is redirected. Whether in the liturgical rites of the early church or the visionary texts of desert fathers, the emphasis was never on evading death, but on preparing to meet it rightly. Not to conquer it, but to walk its path awake.

Even in silence, cultures encode this preparation. The folding of hands, the closing of eyes, the washing of feet, these are not practical gestures. They are directional. They tilt the body toward passage. Toward the idea that something continues, even if we cannot follow it with words.

In this light, death's corridor is not enclosed. It opens, sometimes gently, sometimes with force. But always toward something that calls us forward. The body quiets, but the story does not stop. It flows into other forms. Some remembered, some only guessed. Still, the current moves. And part of us listens.

What We Construct to Cross

We do not know what happens after the last breath. But we try, fiercely, instinctively, to shape the moment that comes before it.

The rituals we create around death are more than comfort for the living. They are temporary architectures, shaped in urgency around a door we sense but cannot enter. When we gather at bedsides, light candles, whisper prayers, or sing hymns over the newly still, we do more than honor a life. We attempt to midwife a crossing.

This impulse is striking in its universality. In the anointing of the sick, the Jewish vidui confessional, the hospice chaplain's whisper of "Go in peace," we speak into that silent space as if something hears. And perhaps something does.

In the Christian tradition, this instinct finds theological grounding in the mystery of Christ's own death. The Gospels do not shield us from his final moments. Jesus cries out. He thirsts. He entrusts his spirit to the Father (Luke 23:46). Then comes a pause, between the last breath and the dawn of resurrection. The Apostles' Creed says, "He descended into hell." Its meaning remains debated, but the phrasing remains. Even the Son of God did not pass straight from death into glory. He went through.

Whatever this passage is, it demands witness. So we build scaffolds.

We construct funerals, obituaries, eulogies, wakes. We dress the body. We write last letters. Some write wills not only to distribute belongings, but to leave behind voice and vision. Small lighthouses to keep the departed tethered to this side a little longer.

These rituals do more than honor the dead. They protect the living from the collapse of narrative. If death is null, if it is nothing, then our stories end mid-sentence. But if death is threshold, then they turn a page.

The turning may be quiet, unresolved, even fearful. Still, it moves. And movement gives grief a direction.

I remember when my grandmother died. In her last days, she was mostly bedridden, barely able to speak. I asked if she wanted to be buried in her brown dress, the one she wore to church and more somber occasions, or the purple one she saved for celebrations and more festive events.

"Brown," she said.

She had already taken care of her burial plans years earlier, but by then, she was hundreds of miles from where they'd been arranged. So after she passed, I busied myself with making local arrangements.

I wrote her eulogy, not just to mark her passing, but to tell the story of who she was before dementia took hold. I wanted people to know the woman I remembered. Whole, sharp, dignified. I wanted them to know my Grandma.

There were no handpicked verses or songs, no tightly choreographed ritual. But there was still intention. In her one-word reply. In the choices I made. In the care behind each act of remembering. She hadn't shaped the threshold in the way some do, but she was still guiding me through it.

The rituals we build do not resolve the mystery. They keep us from falling into it without warning.

Faith does not ask us to explain the void. It asks us to trust that someone meets us there. That even if we cannot see the river, or pierce the veil, or find the gate, a hand reaches back. "Precious in the sight of the Lord is the death of his saints" (Psalm 116:15). Not pitied. Not erased. Precious.

Perhaps what we build, in the end, is not a bridge. It is a witness stand. We gather at the riverbank. We speak the names. We light the lamps. And we wait, without proof, but in search of peace.

To live as if death is a threshold is to live as if love endures.

What we construct at the edge of death may look fragile, but it holds. A folded note. A final prayer. The clasped hand of someone who stays until the end. These are not small things. They are how we hold shape in the face of dissolution.

In some traditions, the dying are invited to speak blessings before they go. It is spoken not to seal the past, but to extend a thread of belonging into the unknown. In others, songs accompany the last breath, not to chase away fear, but to accompany it. Music becomes the boat, the voice the oar.

What we build does not aim for permanence. It forms presence, tangible in the moment that asks us to stay. A presence that says: you are seen. You are accompanied. You are not alone in this final unfolding.

These offerings do not pretend to soften death. But they declare that love has not fled from its threshold. And that declaration matters.

Make a Difference with Your Review

A Small Gesture. A Quiet Light.

> "What is done in love is done well." – Vincent van Gogh

We don't always know the ripple our voice might cause. A small act, a word, a moment, a review, can open a window for someone we'll never meet. It can help them find something they weren't sure they were looking for.

You're here because *Into the Void* means something to you. Maybe it stirred questions that won't quite settle. Maybe it helped you sit with the ache. Or offered language for what you already felt but didn't know how to say.

If that's true, would you leave a review?

It doesn't have to be long. Just honest. A few words that say: *this book met me somewhere real.*

Most readers find books by listening to other readers. That's why your review matters more than you think. It helps someone else, someone curious about what lies between death, time, and eternity, decide if they're ready to go there too.

It takes less than a minute. But it can do something lasting.

Your review could help:
- one more grieving heart find language instead of silence
- one more seeker feel less alone in their questions
- one more person wonder, not fear, what we cannot see

If you're willing, you can leave a review here:

https://www.amazon.com/review/review-your-purchases/?asin=B0F8NZW24P

(Or just scan the QR code below, if you're holding the book.)

Thank you. For reading. For caring. For helping the next soul find their way to the same quiet threshold.

With gratitude,

Renae C. Linde

Chapter Six

CONSCIOUSNESS WITHOUT CLOCKWORK

The Dying Brain and the Stretching Moment

We are told it ends in an instant. One moment we are here, breathing, stitched into the thread of time, and the next, unmade. What if dying does not behave like other moments? What if the exit from time is less a disappearance and more an unraveling?

I remember watching my grandmother die. Her eyes softened. Her hands curled like petals drawing inward. I sat beside her, asking quiet questions, her final wishes. When she whispered "brown," I knew she was still with me.

When her chest rose one last time and fell, something in the room held. Not in minutes or breath counts, but in texture. The space thickened. I had just finished praying over her, reciting scripture through tears.

She was gone. Time didn't stop. It lost its edge.

That strange elasticity, where seconds stretch beyond themselves, is more than a trick of grief. Science suggests the brain may linger after the body collapses. In a 2018 study published in Annals of Neurology, researchers recorded electrical activity in rats after cardiac arrest. The findings startled them: after the heart stopped, the brainwaves didn't fade. They flared. Patterns tied to consciousness surged for as long as thirty seconds after death (Borjigin et al., 2013). Later studies in humans show similar patterns. Near-death experiences often feature the collapse or distortion of time, a flash of memory, a sense of floating, a perception of eternal light.

One theory posits a final surge of neural activity, a "last wave," producing this hyperreal moment (Martial et al., 2021). From a material view, these are dying neurons firing reflexively, like sparks flickering in a darkening house. For those who return from the brink, the moment does not feel mechanical. It feels sacred.

To imagine that moment is to confront perception untethered from sequence. If time fractures rather than ends, could eternity be sensed as a second that refuses to finish?

Inside time, we count in durations. Inside time's collapse, what remains is density. A second can hold lifetimes when the mind loses its grip on forward motion. Some say time slows in crisis. Others say it collapses. In the lab, we can observe distortions: neural loops that stretch moments into decades or erase entire hours. But there are moments science cannot fully chart.

Einstein once wrote to a grieving friend that "the distinction between past, present and future is only a stubbornly persistent illusion" (Einstein, 1955). He wasn't offering comfort. He was pointing to the rupture. Not of life, but of sequence. The scaffolding we trust to hold reality straight may not survive the blink.

In that light, to "experience" anything after death becomes a complex idea. What is experience when there is no sequence? What is a thought without another to follow?

Still, we cling to the possibility that something continues. Consciousness may not vanish like a switch. It may dissolve like a candle melting into the dark, moment by moment, glow by glow, until the wick is gone and yet light still lingers in the air.

There are stories, quiet ones, often dismissed, that speak of moments after death where something unnamed brushes close. A presence. A recognition. In hospital rooms and hospice beds, people describe hearing their names after a loved one has passed, or feeling the weight of a hand on their shoulder though no one else is there. These accounts are difficult to verify, but their consistency points toward a shared intuition: that death does not sever; it thins.

Christian mystics have long held that the veil between worlds is not opaque, only delicate. Gregory of Nyssa wrote of death as the "passage through a narrowing," a movement not toward oblivion but toward transfiguration. In that framework, the dying mind may not hallucinate but begin to see truly, like eyes adjusting to a different kind of light. The surge of neural activity becomes less a malfunction and more a realignment, an opening.

Mythological traditions mirror this. In the Egyptian Book of the Dead, the soul moves through thresholds of judgment and recognition, encountering aspects of self and divinity. In Tibetan Buddhism, the bardo describes an intermediate space, neither alive nor fully departed, where clarity and confusion coexist. These metaphors do not conflict with doctrine; they stretch it, suggesting that what lies beyond is not static but relational. The soul does not exit. It is met.

This meeting, between time-bound perception and what might lie beyond, could explain why near-death experiences are so intensely vivid. Not because they are hallucinations, but because they may briefly anchor both realms. The clarity some report may not be fantasy, but an echo of eternal structure touching temporal collapse.

To dwell on this is not to speculate idly. It is to take seriously the sacredness of thresholds. Theology has always concerned itself with the nature of crossings: from sin to grace, from death to life, from flesh to spirit. And if the mind, in its last act, opens rather than closes, then death itself becomes a sacrament of awareness.

That is the question we face, not whether something happens after, but how we are changed in the passing. Not as aftermath, but as encounter. As revelation. As the first glimpse of a pattern we sensed all along, but could not yet name.

Relativity, Black Holes, and the Perception of Timelessness

In the strange architecture of the cosmos, time is not constant. It bends. It slows. It stalls. Einstein's general theory of relativity revealed that time is interwoven with space, a pliable fabric rather than a fixed rhythm. The closer one moves to intense gravity, the slower time flows. At the edge of a black hole, where gravity peaks and curvature nears infinity, time for the falling object nearly halts. From the outside, it seems frozen at the event horizon, never fully vanishing, never returning.

This is not metaphor. This is physics.

To a distant observer, the falling object appears suspended, caught in the moment of crossing, light stretched red, time arrested. Yet for the object itself, time continues. It moves inward. The contradiction does not signal error. It reveals multiplicity: time changes depending on position and perspective.

Here, science begins to echo something ancient. The biblical imagination has always wrestled with the tension between divine eternity and human time. "With the Lord one day is as a thousand years, and a thousand years as one day" (2 Peter 3:8). This is more than poetic framing. It is a metaphysical disruption. An invitation to loosen our grip on time as absolute and recognize it as experience.

What the physicist calls relativity, the mystic names mystery.

If time can stretch to near-stillness under gravitational force, could the end of a human life, dense with memory, longing, and spirit, create a rupture of its own? Could the moment of death become an interior event horizon, where time dilates so completely that eternity unfolds inward?

Some theologians have considered this. Hans Urs von Balthasar proposed that time in eternity is not erased, but transfigured, like light through stained glass. No longer linear. Still real. In this view, eternity is not measured in endless succession. It is a state in which all is fully present to God.

What the dying may encounter, then, is transformation. A second, split open.

Black holes offer a haunting parallel. Inside, the laws that separate past from future collapse. The final boundary, what physicists call the singularity, cannot be mapped. Not because it hides. Because it defies the coordinates we trust to define reality.

So does death.

We look toward it with equations and scripture, metaphors and models. It absorbs every effort. We are left with approximations.

And awe.

Perhaps awe itself is the only adequate posture. Not resignation, but attentiveness. In both cosmology and faith, the threshold matters more than the answer. When confronted with a singularity, we do not uncover new facts. We meet the limit of human description.

In medieval theology, apophatic language, naming by negation, emerged to express what could not be captured directly. God as infinite, incomprehensible, unbounded. The black hole mirrors this impulse. Its existence is affirmed by what it affects, not by what can be seen. The center cannot be mapped, but its gravity pulls galaxies into orbit. Likewise, the sacred may be more clearly traced by its consequences than by its form.

This does not diminish revelation. It intensifies it. The idea that death, like the singularity, could be a place of collapse and convergence opens a radical theological possibility: that endings are not interruptions. They are convergences of all that has moved toward meaning.

If eternity is not succession but saturation, then the final moment of life, under enough spiritual and emotional gravity, might achieve a kind of total density. Every memory. Every love. Every wound. Compressed into a single awareness. A soul drawn inward not into silence, but into fullness.

Scripture gestures toward this fullness when it speaks of God as "all in all" (1 Corinthians 15:28). Not as distant culmination, but as the interior culmination of everything the soul has become. The paradox of the singularity, impossible to know, yet inescapable in its pull, may teach us to think differently about divine presence. Not far beyond, but deeply within. Not separate from time, but suffusing it until time can hold no more.

This is not the language of certainty. It is the language of reverence. What the mystics preserved, what the physicists discover, and what the dying may glimpse are not fragments of different truths. They are facets of the same unknowable center.

We stand near that center when we listen closely to the questions death asks. Not to answer them, but to feel their weight. Like gravity. Like grace.

And when the moment arrives, whatever it is, we may find ourselves already aligned. Drawn not toward erasure, but toward concentration. The way a star disappears into the singularity and becomes, at last, entirely itself.

Perception as Threshold

It is a strange thing to realize that consciousness may not follow time, but create the bridge that allows it to pass.

Across cultures, the moment of death is imagined as a crossing. The Egyptian Duat, the Greek Styx, the Judeo-Christian Jordan. Whether drawn from myth or scripture, death is rarely described as blankness. It is movement. Transition. A change in perceptual state.

We often mistake perception for duration. If we experience something, we assume it occurred in time. But what if that assumption is the limit?

In neurobiology, perception is interpretive, not reflective. The brain doesn't receive time, it assembles it through contrast, sequence, and rhythm. Remove these cues, and time unravels. The Ganzfeld effect demonstrates this: under sensory deprivation, temporal awareness degrades quickly. Five minutes may feel like fifty. The edges between now and not-now blur (Wackermann et al., 2008).

This is no failure. It unveils. We are shaped for rhythm, yet something in us leans toward what lies beyond it.

In myth, those who cross through death return changed. Their vision alters, even when memory does not accompany them. Orpheus descends for Eurydice and is warned not to look back. The risen Christ appears radiant, unrecognized by those who once knew Him (Luke 24:16). In these stories, perception defines the boundary. What one sees, and the way of seeing, becomes the border between realms.

Even Paul, describing a vision of paradise, admits, "Whether in the body or out of the body I do not know, God knows" (2 Corinthians 12:3). Consciousness detached from bodily time still perceives, without needing sequence to validate what is real.

If perception can exist unanchored from time, then perhaps it is not bound to it. Perhaps it is the threshold itself, rendered porous not by force or revelation, but by the quiet collapse of forward motion.

Mystics have long testified to this strange disassembly. Julian of Norwich described being "lifted into timelessness," where every moment held together, yet nothing was missing (Julian of Norwich, 1373/1998). In the Bhagavad Gita, Arjuna glimpses Krishna in his eternal form, past and future dissolve into overwhelming presence. He falls to his knees, undone by majesty he cannot order.

Perception may be the final sacrament. For what it permits. It shows us how to remain when sequence falls away.

In this framing, the threshold bears no door, no river, no light. It is marked by the release of measurement. A mind freed from clocks and outcomes. A stillness that becomes holy.

What we call death may not end perception. It may change its frame.

No null. No clear threshold.

Just seeing, without when.

If seeing can occur outside duration, then the last vision may not be a final image. It may be a convergence, everything seen at once. Not a memory, not a projection, but a kind of total presence. The mystics do not describe timelessness as absence, but as saturation. Julian's vision was not dimmed; it was overflowing.

This suggests that death may return perception to a state unmediated by before and after. Theologians have long debated whether eternity unfolds as linear afterlife or reorients being altogether. If God is eternally present to all things, then those drawn into divine life may begin to see with the same immediacy. Sequence dissolves. Wholeness remains.

Such seeing requires neither light nor form. It does not resemble vision as we know it; it emerges as recognition, a knowing without unfolding. In the Eastern Orthodox tradition, the hesychasts spoke of a stillness so deep it became luminous, no longer stirred by external revelation, but grounded in interior union. The silence itself became perceptive.

This stillness may be what some near-death experiencers describe: a space that holds them, yet asks nothing. No instruction. No forward path. Just presence. For those immersed in chronos, this sounds like erasure. For those aligned with kairos, sacred time, it feels like return.

If the self dissolves into this field of perception, then the final sacrament is not action, but surrender. To let go of measure requires no vanishing, only alignment with the rhythm that underlies all rhythms. The pulse of being itself.

And this may be the closest our language can come. We do not define what comes after death, we trace what death might reveal. Disappearance dissolves. Arrival fades. What remains is a recalibration of the self toward the unmeasured. Toward the Real.

To prepare for death, then, is to release the script of endings. To loosen the grip on sequence. To learn the art of still perception. To trust that the soul, freed from time's scaffolding, enters no silence, only a clarity long held at the edges of time.

There is no threshold in this clarity. No veil torn. No curtain lifted.

Only perception, finally unlatched from when, becoming what it was always meant to be.

Chapter Seven

WHEN MEMORY CAN'T FOLLOW

Memory and the Soul

What happens to the soul when memory dissolves?

In life, memory is often mistaken for self. We say someone has lost themselves when they forget, when names, rituals, and shared moments vanish from reach. The implication lingers, quiet and heavy: to lose memory is to lose the thread of identity. Yet Christian hope suggests we are more than recollection. What God remembers lasts longer than what we do.

Scripture offers no psychological map of the soul after death. It gives no diagrams of post-mortem memory. But it speaks of being known. "Now I know in part; then I shall know fully, even as I have been fully known" (1 Corinthians 13:12). The paradox sits here: the self that forgets is still held by the One who never does.

Christian theology affirms the soul's immortality as continuity. Thomas Aquinas argued that the soul's intellect and will, not bound to bodily organs, remain beyond death (Summa Theologica, I, q. 75). If the soul persists, it retains something of what it was. But memory, tangled in flesh and synapse, is harder to follow.

Neuroscience tells us memory is temporal and physical. It is not housed in one location, but spread across networks, fragile, rewritable, shaped in every retelling. Memory behaves less like archive and more like story. When the brain dies, the story stops. From a biological view, that is the end.

But theology speaks beyond the circuitry. It imagines a soul not stored in neurons, but remembered in God. "For you formed my inward parts; you knitted me together in my mother's womb… in your book were written, every one of them, the days that were formed for me" (Psalm 139:13, 16). Memory may vanish from awareness. The self remains in God's.

This opens uneasy questions. If I wake in eternity without my memories, without the relational map I've drawn across a lifetime, am I still myself? Or am I someone new, starting over? Can love be recognized without the story that shaped it?

John Locke proposed that personal identity depends on memory. If I do not remember being me, then I am not the same. But this view breaks under the weight of Alzheimer's, amnesia, and death. We know, by love and presence, that identity must go deeper than recall.

In Christian worship, memory is not confined to cognition. It is enacted. The Eucharist, central to liturgical life, does not merely recall Christ's sacrifice, it makes it present. "Do this in remembrance of me" (Luke 22:19) is not an invitation to nostalgic recollection but a call to inhabit a memory God sustains. In this act, believers participate in a truth larger than their ability to mentally retrieve it.

This sacramental memory stands apart from biological memory. It is collective, continuous, and animated by the Spirit. Even when personal memory fades, the Church remembers. In the prayers, in the creeds, in the seasons of the liturgical year, memory is preserved not as data but as presence. Here, the soul is not lost when it forgets; it is still found in the Body.

This is not theoretical comfort. It is ontological grounding. The baptized are not remembered because they recall. They are remembered because they belong. The memory of the Church does not depend on the brain's networks but on a communion that transcends death.

Here, Christian doctrine resists reduction. It insists that what is most vital is not subject to entropy. If our stories collapse under the weight of time, grace does not. If the self becomes unmoored in dementia, liturgy still names and gathers it. Memory, in this sense, is not a possession but a promise. The promise that no soul will be forgotten by the One who called it into being.

Memory, in its fragility, often dictates our perception of self. Yet, when stripped away, by age, trauma, or death, what remains? The Christian tradition offers a perspective: that our essence is preserved not in our recollections but in being known by God. The Apostle Paul writes, "Now I know in part; then I shall know fully, even as I have been fully known" (1 Corinthians 13:12). This suggests a continuity of self that transcends our earthly memories. Thomas Aquinas further posits that the soul's intellect and will persist beyond death, independent of the physical brain (Summa Theologica, I, q. 75).

Neuroscience corroborates the impermanence of memory. Studies indicate that memories are not static imprints but dynamic, distributed networks susceptible to alteration and decay. The case of Henry Molaison, who lost the ability to form new memories after surgery, underscores the brain's role in memory and identity. Yet, even without new memories, Molaison retained a sense of self, hinting at an identity beyond mere recollection.

This intersection of theology and science invites reflection: if our memories fade, does our identity dissolve? Or is there a deeper anchor? Christian doctrine suggests that our true self is held in the divine memory, untainted by the erosion of time. This belief offers solace, asserting that even in forgetfulness, we are remembered.

Greek mythology offers more than a cautionary tale about forgetting. It offers tension. In some traditions, souls drink from Lethe to forget earthly life. In others, they choose Mnemosyne, remembrance, to awaken something eternal. These rivers form more than underworld geography; they mirror our deepest question: is love preserved through memory, or does it endure in spite of it?

In personal experience, witnessing a loved one's memory fade due to illness challenges our understanding of self. Still, moments of clarity or recognition suggest that the core identity endures. These glimpses affirm the belief that the soul remains intact, even when memory falters.

Christian eschatology does not merely anticipate survival; it anticipates vindication. The final judgment is not an audit of recollections, but a reckoning that restores what was broken, including what memory alone cannot hold. Scripture speaks of books opened (Revelation 20:12), not as ledgers of guilt, but as records of a life seen completely, perhaps even more truthfully than we saw it ourselves.

This raises a further hope: that the memory of God is not only perfect but redemptive. The injustices forgotten by victims, the moments misunderstood even by those who lived them, do not vanish into silence. They are kept, clarified, and, ultimately, transfigured. What we failed to articulate in our lifetime does not remain unspoken in God's eternity.

This eschatological memory is not punitive. It is restorative. It does not trap the soul in a past it can no longer amend. Rather, it frees the soul by locating it fully within a justice that holds nothing lightly, and nothing forever against us. Memory, in divine hands, becomes the ground of mercy. What is remembered is not simply what occurred, but what it meant.

In this way, Christian doctrine draws a sharp contrast with materialist despair. If death ends the story, memory's collapse is a final erasure. But if God remembers rightly, the story's truth survives even where our version did not. In God's memory, no part is lost, only completed.

Thus, while memory shapes our earthly identity, it is not the sole custodian of self. In the Christian view, our essence is preserved in God's eternal memory, offering hope that we remain whole, even as our recollections wane.

Paul alludes to this mystery: "We shall all be changed, in a moment, in the twinkling of an eye" (1 Corinthians 15:52). A transformation. The soul, in Christian imagination, does not remain fixed. It lives. It is refined. It can be joined to something beyond what it once understood. If memory cannot follow, perhaps love can. Perhaps the self is tied not to what it can retrieve, but to who it is held by.

Here science and faith diverge. Neuroscience ends where neurons do. Theology continues with what is given to God. Yet both hint at the same truth: memory is a fragile keeper. Continuity may live elsewhere, in where we are received.

If memory cannot cross the void, something else must carry us.
Something unrecorded.
Something remembered.

Reuniting Without Remembering

If heaven holds reunion without memory, what is it we return to?

The idea of reunion runs deep in the Christian imagination. We speak of seeing loved ones again, of being gathered into a great cloud of witnesses, of feasting at the marriage supper of the Lamb (Revelation 19:9). The longing stretches beyond God, it reaches toward one another. Grief, too, often aches with unfinished conversations and untouchable faces. But if, as explored earlier, memory cannot pass through the veil unaltered, a theological tension rises: can love endure without the story that shaped it?

The Gospels offer no clear doctrine on post-mortem memory, but their silence may guide us. When Mary Magdalene meets the risen Christ, she doesn't recognize him, until he speaks her name (John 20:16). The recognition is not summoned from memory. It comes from something deeper. It is not summoned through thought. It arises through intimacy. A knowing beneath recollection.

Scripture portrays love as something more than recognition. "Love never ends" (1 Corinthians 13:8). Its permanence does not rest on memory. It flows from God, who is love (1 John 4:8). If reunion depends on shared memory, it breaks easily. If it arises from divine love, it holds. We may not be the ones who remember. We may be the ones remembered.

Other traditions echo this paradox. Norse cosmology describes memory fading in the mist. In the Bardo Thödol, the Tibetan Book of the Dead, the soul traverses thresholds shaped not by memory, but by transformation.

Christian thought resists this forgetting in its cyclical form, but it does not promise the preservation of memory as we know it.

It hints at something changed: "The former things shall not be remembered or come into mind" (Isaiah 65:17). It is not a loss, but a loosening. It is not that love is erased, but that its limits are lifted.

But then what of the mother who longs to see her child? The husband who carries his wife's laugh like breath? The sister, the friend, the beloved? If we rise into eternity without these echoes, is reunion still reunion?

Here, myth and theology meet again, not to define, but to evoke. Jewish mystics describe the soul's return to the Olam HaBa, the World to Come, as a reunion not with companions, but with the divine source from which all souls arise. In this vision, love is not maintained in its prior form. It reaches completion in union. We do not find those we loved by tracking old patterns. We return to the Love in which we once met them.

And still, the ache remains. We want to be known by name. Not dissolved. Not generalized. Christianity affirms this desire. It insists on the resurrection of the body, the persistence of personhood, the sanctity of the saints. But it also speaks of change, of being clothed in incorruptibility (1 Corinthians 15:53). A transformation so profound it may lift us beyond the need for former knowing. Not erased. Transcended.

There is mercy in that. That bonds formed in time may endure even without recall. That in the light of eternity, recognition could be immediate, not retrieved, but given.

Perhaps this is where the liturgy speaks most powerfully, not as repetition, but as reentry. In Eucharist, baptism, benediction, we return to the same words not to remember with accuracy, but to remember with presence. These acts rehearse belonging until it becomes real, not through recollection but through participation. The soul is shaped in the rhythm, even when the reason escapes it.

Communal memory, unlike personal memory, does not depend on cognition. It depends on practice. A child who forgets the creed still belongs to the people who recite it. A widow who cannot recall the hymns still rests inside the music that carried her for decades. These patterns hold the self when the self cannot hold itself.

In this way, reunion may not hinge on mutual recognition but on mutual rootedness, in God, in worship, in the mystery of being held. Eternity does not require us to reassemble what was lost. It reveals what never left.

To be known beyond remembering.

To be loved without recounting.

To be reunited by origin, not sequence.

The Risk of Resurrection

We speak of resurrection as comfort. But it carries risk.

To be raised, not merely restored, requires surrender. Everything we think defines us must be laid down. Resurrection does not rewind death. It does not reverse time. It is no miracle of memory. It is re-creation. A making-new that transcends biology and biography. "Behold, I am making all things new," says the One enthroned in Revelation (21:5). But if I am among those things made new, if even the self is reconstituted, who then rises?

The Gospels do not soften this tension. When Jesus rises, he is himself, and changed. His followers do not know him on the road to Emmaus. His body still bears scars, yet moves through walls. He eats broiled fish, yet ascends. Resurrection here is not resuscitation. It is transfiguration. The implication is clear: resurrection alters not only our condition, but our core.

In quieter moments, I ask: would I know myself beyond the veil? Would the one who rises feel continuous with the one who wept in hospital corridors, or curled under blankets in doubt? Would the self shaped by anxiety, by love, by all the imperfect tenderness of this world still remain, or would it dissolve in the light?

And if I no longer fear, am I still me? If I forget my child's first cry, my mother's hand, what remains of the shape those memories etched in me?

Paul writes, "It is sown a natural body; it is raised a spiritual body" (1 Corinthians 15:44). But what does that mean? What does a spiritual body keep? What must it release? Christian theology insists on embodiment. Resurrection affirms a body, not a vapor. Yet the resurrected self escapes decay, escapes time, escapes history. It is no longer confined to the self that suffered, hoped, or failed. This is the risk: that the "you" who once lived may vanish into the person you were always meant to become.

Other faiths echo this surrender. In Eastern traditions, enlightenment dissolves illusion. The self quiets. The small narrative ends. In mystical Judaism, tikkun ha-nefesh may span lifetimes, each one erasing the last, until only the divine essence remains. Even in Lewis's The Great Divorce, the soul must lay down its old affections to stand in heaven's brightness.

So what does resurrection promise? That you will return as yourself? Or that you will rise beyond yourself?

Isaiah declares: "Your dead shall live; their bodies shall rise. You who dwell in the dust, awake and sing for joy!" (Isaiah 26:19). I want to believe it. I do believe it. But sometimes I wonder: does joy ask us to release everything that once made us small, everything we once called ours?

Perhaps this is what Christ meant when he said, "Whoever would save his life will lose it, and whoever loses his life for my sake will find it" (Matthew 16:25). Not the end of existence. The surrender of identity as possession. The death of self-definition. Then, resurrection.

This is not sentiment. It is holy disassembly.

You do not return to who you were.

The unveiling of who you have always been.

To rise is to risk never coming back the same.

To rise is to become who you are in God.

What if resurrection means arriving as a stranger to ourselves? Or worse, to those we love? It is one thing to rise glorious. It is another to be unrecognizable.

Gregory of Nyssa imagined resurrection not as a static return, but as an infinite unfolding into the divine likeness. Each soul, he said, moves "from glory to glory," endlessly transfigured. In this view, there is no fixed identity to retrieve, only a deepening into God's image. The self is not preserved like a relic. It is drawn forward, refined past familiarity.

This confounds our longing for reunion. We do not want abstractions. We want the faces we kissed, the hands we held. We want them whole, yes, but also the same. We do not want to love someone new. We want to love again the ones we already lost.

But even in Scripture, recognition fails. Mary does not know Jesus until he speaks her name. The disciples on the shore think him a ghost until he breaks bread. The resurrected One is not what they expect. He is more. His presence reorders their memory of him. Not replacement, not amnesia, but a fullness too large for prior comprehension.

This may be our future, too. We will know, and not know. We will remember, and be remade. We may not find each other as we were. But we may know one another as we were always meant to be.

This is not the erasure of history. It is its transfiguration. What was done in weakness is raised in strength. What was loved in part may be received in whole. The story is not discarded. It is fulfilled.

Still, it troubles. The self I know, even with its failures, is the only one I can imagine rising. But resurrection is not the continuation of life as we knew it. It is its consummation. The seed bears no resemblance to the tree, Paul writes. Yet the tree comes from the seed.

This is why resurrection cannot be owned. It must be received. It is gift, not guarantee. It is the final undoing of control.

And in that undoing, perhaps the greatest mercy: the loss of every illusion we mistook for permanence. The shedding of every version of ourselves we thought we had to defend.

Here lies the difference between immortality and resurrection. Immortality extends what already is. Resurrection transforms it. One clings to identity. The other opens to mystery.

In the end, resurrection does not promise that you will be as you were. It promises that you will be as God sees you.

Chapter Eight

The Trouble with Knowing

Mystery as Mercy

There is mercy in not knowing. To see it that way, something in us must die.

We enter a world that gives us answers before we know how to ask. Childhood is filled with certainties handed down: God is good, the soul endures, everything has a reason. These are meant to comfort, to steady us. What happens when the questions grow larger than the answers? When death stops feeling like a doorway and begins to feel like a disappearance?

It starts with a fracture. A loss that refuses to follow the rules. A silence so thick it ceases to feel sacred. It may come through grief, doubt, or the slow disintegration of confidence in the stories we once trusted. Here we reach the edge of mystery, as those staring into silence.

The instinct is to rescue ourselves with meaning. Scripture models something else. In the storm of Job's anguish, when every plea demanded an explanation, God did not offer clarity. He offered presence, veiled in power. "Where were you when I laid the foundation of the earth?" (Job 38:4). The reply was an invitation to release control.

Job's unknowing was not condemned. It was consecrated. He was asked to behold.

This is surrender, a surrender of control. A readiness to kneel. Some truths are too vast for our frame, too sacred for words.

Paul gestures toward this when he writes, "For now we see in a mirror dimly, but then face to face" (1 Corinthians 13:12). Dimness is the condition of faith. We live by partial light.

Mystery is what belief breathes.

If that is so, then perhaps the truest sign of spiritual maturity is consent. A willingness to yield to the unknown without treating it as lack. A posture of reverence.

For me, the sharpest encounter with unknowing came after losing someone I loved without boundary. No vision came. No voice. Just silence. But I did not feel forsaken. I felt the vacancy of what had left. The hollow echo of absence where once there had been consciousness. The body remained, but it was no longer inhabited. Something sacred had departed without explanation, and what remained bore its silence like a weight.

Over time, I came to understand that silence as restraint. What could have been said would have shattered. No explanation could meet the scale of loss. Perhaps the mercy was this: I was not summoned to interpret death. I was asked to stay with it. To bear witness. And to trust that the One who spun galaxies does not blink in the face of absence.

If God is real, and I believe He is, then His silence is not vacancy. It is fullness waiting for the right time.

We often treat mystery as error to be corrected. The sacred texts resist this. The Psalmist writes, "Such knowledge is too wonderful for me; it is high; I cannot attain it" (Psalm 139:6). This is not despair. It is devotion.

There is holiness in limits. Grace in the unanswered.

And perhaps the most enduring truth is this:

What cannot be known was never meant for knowing.

It was meant for kneeling.

Yet even kneeling is not passive. To kneel before what we cannot comprehend is to enter into the discipline of reverence. It is to take a form that allows the soul to speak without needing to be heard. Faith, in this light, becomes less a system of answers than a sustained consent to live within questions that resist resolution.

The ancient mystics knew this. Gregory of Nyssa described the spiritual journey as one of "infinite progress," a perpetual movement into the darkness of God's unseeable light. The closer the soul draws, the more it recognizes the vastness of what remains hidden. This is not regression. It is purification, a stripping of every idol fashioned in the image of certainty.

Our era recoils from this. We prize knowledge as mastery. We confuse information with intimacy. Even our spiritual practices are often designed to produce clarity, to deliver insight on demand. But revelation cannot be engineered. The cloud of unknowing is not an obstacle to be removed; it is the habitat of the holy.

Christ himself embodied this. At the heart of the crucifixion is not a doctrine but a silence. "My God, my God, why have you forsaken me?" (Matthew 27:46). These are not words of doubt. They are the cry of a soul immersed in the full mystery of divine withdrawal. And yet in that darkness, redemption unfolds. It offers no explanation, but is as an event. The veil tears. The earth shakes.

The dead rise. All this happens not through understanding, but through obedience to the silence.

To love God in the absence of answers is to love without bargaining. It is to give ourselves without condition, even when what we receive is absence itself. The early Church fathers called this apatheia, the quieting of the soul's demand for control. A holy stillness that waits without rush, trusts without proof.

In the contemplative tradition, this waiting is essential. The Desert Fathers did not flee into solitude to escape the world. They went to be stripped of illusions. Their silence was attentiveness, honed over time. A readiness to receive whatever came, without needing it to resolve.

We lose this posture when we treat mystery as a problem to solve. When the unknown becomes unbearable, we fill the void with answers we have not earned. But wisdom grows more in relinquishment than in achievement. The Psalms speak to this again and again. "I have calmed and quieted my soul, like a weaned child with its mother" (Psalm 131:2). There is no striving in that image. No conquest. Only belonging.

This belonging does not remove pain. It reframes it. To grieve with God is not an escape from sorrow. It sanctifies it. The sorrow remains, but it is no longer alone. It becomes a meeting place. A thin space. In grief, the heart breaks open, and into that opening comes a Presence too large for speech.

We do not always recognize it as Presence. Sometimes it arrives as stillness. Sometimes as the soft ache of beauty that does not explain but reminds. We feel it in the echo of ancient prayers, in the pages of sacred texts that read us while we read them, in the quiet loyalty of those who stay beside us without speaking. In these moments, the silence becomes its own language.

That language does not translate well into systems. It resists theology as concept and returns us to theology as encounter. This is where the mystics dwell, not in abstraction, but in the ache of what cannot be tamed. Meister Eckhart writes, "God is not found in the soul by adding anything, but by a process of subtraction." We do not approach the divine by accumulation. We approach by letting go.

This letting go is not despair. It is the surrender of false hope. A hope built on resolution, on making sense, will collapse under the weight of reality. But a hope grounded in presence, however veiled, endures. This is the hope that carried Job. Not that he would understand, but that he would be upheld.

Here, the posture of kneeling becomes not a single act but a sustained orientation. A way of moving through the world with reverence, even when we do not feel reverent. Especially then. To kneel is to remember that we are not God. It is to practice trust in what exceeds us.

This kind of trust does not protect us from loss. It deepens our capacity to bear it. It gives us the strength to remain faithful in the void, to choose love without clarity, to keep walking when the path dissolves beneath our feet.

In this light, mystery is not merely tolerated. It becomes sacred ground. To live by faith is to live inside a truth we do not possess. A truth that possesses us.

And so we kneel, not as an escape from doubt, nor to claim certainty, but because we belong to what exceeds us. We do not dissect mystery; we enter it. We let it shape us.

In the end, knowledge does not hold us. It is love. And love, at its deepest, does not demand comprehension. It endures where meaning falters.

The Illusion of Comprehension

We build our frameworks with care.

Neuroscience gives us language, synapses, structures. Theology gives us creeds. Myth offers symbols. Each attempts to sketch the infinite in terms the finite can bear. They provide scaffolding without claiming the shape of reality itself.

The brain, remarkable as it is, depends on structure. Evolution trained it to seek patterns, impose order, and collapse vastness into forms it can use. This isn't error. It's adaptation.

But story has a limit.

We imagine that with time, training, or devotion, we might stretch far enough to meet the divine. But biology hems us in. Cognitive scientist Donald Hoffman argues that evolution favors usefulness over accuracy. What we perceive is not raw reality, but a survival-optimized interface (Hoffman, 2019). The world we think we see may be more functional than true.

Physics offers no firmer ground. Time, which feels stable, warps under gravity. It slows. It folds. Near black holes, it disintegrates. What does it mean if the very medium through which we live cannot hold form?

Even mathematics, which appears impervious, carries its own wound. Gödel's incompleteness theorems proved that no system can prove all truths about itself (Nagel & Newman, 2001). Some truths can only be seen from elsewhere.

This is not just a collapse in theory. It is a collapse in spirit.

The Tower of Babel was never just about language. It warned against comprehension that refuses surrender. "Let us make a name for ourselves," the builders said (Genesis 11:4). The tower didn't exalt God. It exalted understanding. And it crumbled.

THE TROUBLE WITH KNOWING

Its fall wasn't rage. It was restraint. A mercy that broke the illusion of control.

Mystic traditions have long recognized this kind of collapse as a beginning. The Desert Fathers. The Sufi poets. The Zen masters. They speak of disintegration as the first glimpse of reality. When the framework fails, the ground appears.

That failure rarely feels kind.

We have learned to confuse knowing with security. So when explanations fail, when prayer reverberates into nothing, when doctrine loses its grip, we scramble. We construct again. We draft another map.

But there are moments when the sacred does not respond to comprehension. Not because it hides, but because it cannot be approached directly.

Moses was not shown God's face. He was shown the passing back (Exodus 33:23). That withholding was not distance. It was protection.

So we are given riddles. Visions. Parables. Not to obscure truth, but to prepare us for it.

To be human is to live between image and reality. Between shadow and flame. We speak of God in fragments, light, rock, lion, lamb. They point. They do not define.

We do not see God.

We see the trace.

In time, every scaffold fails. Diagrams fade. Even sacred systems begin to crack. This is not faith collapsing. This is faith shedding its brace so it can breathe.

Truth remains.

But it arrives differently. It does not declare itself through proofs. It appears in presence.

To receive truth as presence is to abandon control. The center of faith shifts from explanation to encounter. And encounter does not extract. It allows.

This does not discard intellect. It relocates it. The mind becomes a lamp. It can offer light. It cannot command revelation.

When Moses came down from the mountain, his face was radiant, and he did not know it (Exodus 34:29). He carried the law, but it was the nearness that changed him. Not the tablets. The presence.

That nearness is the thread that runs through the entire arc of Scripture. God with Adam. With Israel. With Christ. With the Church. The scandal of the Christian claim is not that we understand God, but that God approaches.

And still, the mystery holds. Proximity does not collapse it. It sharpens it. To come closer is to lose the illusion of clarity.

Jesus practiced this deliberately. He answered questions with stories. He described the kingdom in seed and soil and children. He gestured. He did not distill.

The truth was not out of reach. It was too whole to fracture into explanation. Like manna, it was only useful when received anew.

We long for the eternal to be captured. Preserved. Summoned. But the sacred does not submit to ownership. It incinerates our grip. It will not be held.

In Isaiah's vision, the thresholds shake under the cry "Holy, holy, holy" (Isaiah 6:3-4). Holiness is not gentle. It dismantles. The prophet does not celebrate. He confesses: "Woe is me, for I am undone."

And yet, from that undoing comes purpose. The fire purifies. The coal prepares.

This is the rhythm we inherit: encounter, disintegration, sending. It obeys no formula. It operates by grace.

And grace does not request understanding. It invites fidelity. It dares us to remain in mystery without resolution. It offers refinement without clarity.

In spiritual direction, this posture has a name: the discipline of not-knowing. It is a shared stillness that resists interpretation. Both director and directee inhabit the now. They listen not for answers, but for emergence. This is holy ground. Not because it is certain. Because it is honest.

This discipline mirrors the logic of the Incarnation. Christ does not arrive as a conclusion. He arrives in flesh. Tangible. Local. Mortal. The Word does not resolve abstraction. The Word becomes body.

And that body is broken. Buried. Raised.

Even resurrection resists simplification. Christ is mistaken for a stranger. He vanishes mid-meal. He speaks, but carries wounds. The coherence does not return. The mystery intensifies.

And yet, there is weight to it. Not intellectual weight. Existential weight. A new kind of gravity that makes the ground under our feet feel real again.

To live this way is to let go of much. We lose the illusion of control, the security of formula. But in what remains, something deeper forms. A God ungrasped, yet unmistakably encountered. A faith that does not demand defense because it is rooted in love.

The earliest believers called this movement "the Way." They understood what it was. Not a thesis. A path. Something that unfolds only as it is walked.

To walk it is to accept obscurity as part of illumination. It is to pray for communion, not comprehension. It is to approach Scripture as presence, not problem. It is to sit with silence, not as retreat, but as reverence.

And there, everything begins to change. Not quickly. Not loudly. But deeply.

When Paul writes that we are "being transformed into the same image from one degree of glory to another" (2 Corinthians 3:18), he names a process that cannot be engineered. Only received.

Received in the wilderness. In the ache. In the unraveling of once-reliable answers. In the pages that once offered comfort and now offer only stillness.

The wilderness is not exile. It is instruction. It burns away the false and leaves what can bear fire.

And what endures is presence.

This is the orbit we keep tracing. Every story, every ritual, every sacred act draws us back to the One who will not be mapped, yet meets us anyway.

We do not fully know.

But we are held.

And so we stay. We tend the flame. We learn to wait.

Not from fear.

From devotion.

The Faithful Agnostic

Faith and certainty are distinct.

Mystics and prophets have long carried this truth, though it unsettles those shaped by systems that prioritize doctrinal precision. Belief does not grow from explanation. It begins in consent.

To live as a faithful agnostic is to recognize that God may remain beyond the reach of definition. It is to honor what resists language and to trust that silence can bear the weight of presence as fully as any word ever could.

In its earliest use, agnosticism held no indifference. It was humility, a boundary drawn in reverence. Thomas Henry Huxley coined the term to name this restraint, acknowledging that metaphysical reality might outrun the reach of empirical method. But the stance itself predates the word. It lives in Scripture.

Abraham followed a voice without evidence.

Jacob limped from a night he couldn't name.

Mary stood before the impossible and answered, "Let it be to me according to your word" (Luke 1:38).

This is not faith in retreat. It is faith stripped down to what endures.

In myth, divinity rarely arrives with credentials. The gods wear fur, or wind, or the faces of strangers. Their intent is not to mislead, but to measure attention. Odysseus walks beside Athena and never sees. Abraham receives three visitors and only later understands who they were. Revelation belongs to those who no longer require recognition to remain attentive.

Uncertainty has its own sacred function. It dismantles performance. It dissolves argument. It exposes what is left when certainty dissolves. When no creed stands firm, no image holds, what remains alive in us? Do we still reach? Still pray, even when the silence stays?

This is the shape of faithful agnosticism:

To kneel when all names fall short.

To love a God who remains veiled.

To trust the force that set stars into motion to uphold us without needing our comprehension.

If faith sometimes ignites in shadow, maybe that's where its glow becomes visible.

I've prayed into silence. I've looked toward the sky and said, "If You are there, this quiet belongs to You." Still I return to prayer.

Still I whisper into the dark, and at times I even shout to be heard. The longing doesn't come from certainty. It rises from a hunger that never quiets.

Drawn toward something without form. Not resolution. Nearness.

Drawn toward the mystery that remains even as meaning unravels.

The faithful agnostic continues with empty hands. There is no gripping. No display. No demand for closure. Only the steady hope that if God exists, He does not collapse. That if eternity holds, its weight is not ours to engineer.

We were never given the task of charting the void.

Only the invitation to move through it.

✦ Interlude: Through What Cannot Be Marked

There is no flag in the void. No marker that says: You have passed.

We want death to announce itself, to act like a gate, or at least a visible threshold. But maybe thresholds only appear after we've crossed them.

Part II does not offer conclusions. It names the gestures we make in their absence, rivers, veils, blinks, resurrections, silence. We speak of what we cannot see because the ache insists on witness.

We've traced how time distorts at death's edge. How memory falters. How the frames we've trusted splinter under mystery. That splintering may carry grace.

To pass through the void is to stop requiring answers. Not to forsake meaning, but to bow before a scale of meaning we were never meant to hold alone.

Let this be the gift of unknowing: we no longer bear the burden of naming what sustains us.

We need only trust that we are, somehow, sustained.

PART III: BEYOND THE VOID

Living, Loving, and Letting Go While We Still Tick

Chapter Nine

PREPARING FOR THE BLINK

Mortality as a Spiritual Practice

There is a quiet discipline in learning how to die before we die. A sacred loosening. A practiced release of what was never ours to hold.

Christian tradition has carried this truth in the marrow of its liturgy. "Remember that you are dust, and to dust you shall return" (Genesis 3:19). These words, spoken over ash-marked foreheads, are invitations. To remember that we are passing through. To let the daily diminishment of ego, control, ambition, and image become tutors in surrender.

This may be the scandal behind Jesus' command in Luke 9:23: "If anyone would come after me, let him deny himself and take up his cross daily and follow me." The cross was never shorthand for difficulty. It marked public death. And here it becomes a rhythm. A daily movement into relinquishment. A sustained posture of release.

Memento mori, the monastic discipline of remembering death, was a commitment to presence. The skull etched into a ring or placed beside a candle centered the heart. It reminded the beholder that ego is brittle, permanence a mirage. To remember death is to see more clearly. To walk more gently. To let each moment hold its own finite dignity.

Science too, without sentiment, affirms our fragility. Cells die and renew. Bodies bend toward decay. The Second Law of Thermodynamics tells us that systems drift toward disorder. Yet even this becomes a summons to reverence. Mortality is not a flaw in the code. It is the foundation of the design.

Still, we resist. The smaller invitations to release.

I've sensed it in myself. In rituals of postponement. Saving the good dishes. Delaying joy. Hoarding time as if I might spend it later. I've rushed goodbyes. I've lived under the illusion that there will be another morning for whatever I've deferred. The subtext of modern life says, "later, elsewhere." Yet Scripture offers no such buffer: "You do not know what tomorrow will bring... For you are a mist that appears for a little time and then vanishes" (James 4:14).

To practice mortality is to unlearn the demand for certainty.

The saints and mystics welcomed death's nearness as a lens. Saint Benedict instructed his followers to "keep death daily before your eyes." Saint Francis called it Sister Death because it revealed something sacred. Even Christ, in Gethsemane, did not bypass the ache. He sweat blood (Luke 22:44). He faced death with full presence.

There is no formula for this. Only readiness. Only repetition.

You will lose things. Time. Roles. Bodies. People. Ways of meaning. This is not retribution. It is the shape of the life we are given. The shape of the cross. To meet it with reverence may be the truest act of praise.

Living Without Clinging

There's an ache in our grip. A tension between how tightly we hold titles, routines, names, futures, and how little control we possess. Modern life praises mastery, but the soul seems attuned to something gentler. Something that moves through release.

Myths across cultures recognize this. Those who pass through thresholds are rarely the ones who cling. They are the ones who let go. Or are stripped of what once defined them.

In the Sumerian tale of Inanna's descent, the queen of heaven approaches the underworld and must remove a piece of regalia at each of the seven gates. Her crown. Her earrings. Her necklace. Each item falls away until she stands exposed before death. The ritual shames and sanctifies. Transformation becomes possible through that exposure.

In Buddhist teaching, clinging, upādāna, is named as a root of suffering. Refusal amplifies pain. We hold identity, pleasure, doctrine, even our constructed selves as if they were life rafts. But what saves us isn't built from these fragments. What carries us forward arrives when we let the water close over us.

Jesus names this same rhythm: "Whoever finds his life will lose it, and whoever loses his life for my sake will find it" (Matthew 10:39). This is spiritual architecture. Holding tightly preserves nothing. Joining the movement of becoming invites life to endure.

But what does that look like on a weekday?

Loosening begins in habit. In choosing not to over-script a moment. In stepping back from the compulsion to name ourselves too precisely. It unfolds in choosing presence instead of performance. In offering truth instead of polish. This is a refusal to confuse intention with authority.

Physics affirms this. At the quantum level, uncertainty is unavoidable. The Heisenberg principle makes clear: the more precisely we measure one aspect of a particle, the less we can know about another. To fix one truth is to blur another. Observation shapes outcome. Measurement alters being. Reality does not reward grip.

Still, we chase control. Because plans look like purpose. Because even a brittle identity feels safer than emptiness.

And yet, the invitation remains.

The mystics called it kenosis, self-emptying. Not as negation, but as offering. In Philippians 2:7, we're told Christ "emptied himself, taking the form of a servant." Descent, not defensiveness. This is a daily posture. Release what hardens you. Let yourself be reshaped.

This doesn't mean abandoning structure or desire. It means trusting a root system that goes deeper than performance. One that does not require applause to validate its fruit.

I remember a spring when everything I'd built began to unravel. Projects collapsed. Roles thinned. My calendar emptied of direction. At first, I panicked. Then I stood still. Then I listened. The noise of grasping quieted. What remained was attention. I could finally hear the One who never needed my credentials.

This isn't a system. It won't oppose ambition or planning. It asks for a posture. Hold your life as you would water. Let it rise and fall. Let your hands stay open.

Myth teaches that shores never yield passage. Theology shows a kingdom shaped by yielding. And science, in its precision, confesses: control is no synonym for truth.

Joy as Resistance to Finality

There are days when joy feels like disobedience.

Something quieter. Something more stubborn. A refusal to let death speak the final word, even knowing it eventually speaks to everything.

After a recent funeral for a friend, I stepped outside for some air. It wasn't quite spring, but the air felt warm. Trees and flowers were budding. Birds were singing. Traffic moved like a well-oiled machine. Nothing paused. Life persisted, insisting on itself.

Joy, in that moment, wasn't comfort. It was defiance.

To receive beauty in the face of loss is a kind of honoring. A gesture toward the shape of life the dead no longer carry.

Scripture never separates mourning and gladness cleanly. They brush against each other constantly. Ecclesiastes speaks of weeping and laughter, mourning and dancing, as one life, textured by both (Ecclesiastes 3:4). Even in the shadow of Gethsemane, Jesus offered joy. "These things I have spoken to you, that my joy may be in you..." (John 15:11). This is joy rooted in nearness.

It's not just an emotion. It's a stance.

We're not told to be joyful because all is well. We're told to pay attention. To sit at a bedside and laugh. To plant something. To sing while stirring soup. To dance on the kitchen tile where grief once stood.

In myth, joy is often the prize at the end. But what if it's the means?

In Norse mythology, after Ragnarök ends the world, two humans survive hidden inside the World Tree. When they emerge, they laugh. That laughter begins the next age.

In the Hebrew Scriptures, joy is a command given to people still living in ruin. "Do not be grieved," says Nehemiah, "for the joy of the Lord is your strength" (Nehemiah 8:10). A kind of power. A way to remain.

Even neuroscience agrees. Awe and delight, gratitude and play, all soften the grip of fear. They do not silence mortality. But they remind the nervous system that life is more than threat. There is wonder too.

When we live as those who know we're dying, joy becomes faithful.

We don't wait for stability to make something beautiful. We don't postpone joy until permanence arrives. Eternity never asked us to skip the pleasures of now. If death comes unannounced, then joy is the light we leave on.

I think of the woman in hospice who wore lipstick and earrings until her last breath. The widower who kept cooking meals in a quiet house. The child planting daffodils near a small grave. These were gestures. Acts of memory. Acts of courage.

We go on, because we've stopped needing an answer.

Preparing for death includes loosening our grip. But it also means welcoming joy. Even when it flickers. Even when it's brief. Even when we know it cannot cross with us.

Even when we know we must one day close our eyes. And go.

The Descent and the Liminal

In the quiet hours before dawn, when the world holds its breath, I occasionally sit in contemplation, embracing the stillness that precedes the day's chaos. These moments are deliberate descents into the depths of my being, confronting the impermanence that shadows every breath.

The early Christian monks understood this practice well. Their days were punctuated by the *Divine Office*, prayers that acknowledged the transient nature of life and the eternal presence of the Divine. Each chant, each psalm, was a step into the underworld of the soul, a confrontation with mortality that led to spiritual renewal.

This rhythm of descent and ascent mirrors the journey of Inanna, the Sumerian goddess who ventured into the underworld, shedding her worldly adornments at each gate. Her story is not just myth but metaphor, illustrating the necessity of releasing our attachments to encounter the sacred. Inanna's descent is a template for transformation, a path that requires vulnerability and surrender.

The liminal spaces, the thresholds between life and death, certainty and doubt, are where transformation occurs. In these in-between places, we are stripped of our illusions, confronted with the rawness of existence. It's in the hospital waiting rooms, the moments after a loved one's passing, or the silence following a life-altering decision that we find ourselves in the liminal.

These spaces are sacred. They are the crucibles where our souls are refined, where we learn to let go and trust in the unfolding mystery. The mystics called this process *kenosis*, the self-emptying that allows for divine infilling. It's not about erasing the self but about making room for something greater.

Letting go is a continuous practice, rather than a one-time act. It's in the daily choices to release control, to forgive, to embrace uncertainty. It's in the decision to listen deeply, to be present, to love without guarantees.

This practice is echoed in the teachings of Jesus, who invited his followers to take up their crosses daily. The cross, a symbol of death, becomes a symbol of life when embraced willingly. It's in the surrender that we find freedom, in the dying that we find resurrection.

Amidst the acknowledgment of death, joy emerges as a deliberate, faithful stance against despair or finality. It's a refusal to let grief erase beauty. It's the laughter shared at a funeral, the beauty noticed in a decaying leaf, the love expressed in the face of loss. Joy becomes an act of resistance, a declaration that life, even in its fragility, is worth celebrating.

The Apostle Paul wrote of being sorrowful yet always rejoicing, capturing the paradox of the Christian life. It's a life that holds tension, that embraces both mourning and dancing, recognizing that both are integral to the human experience.

To live with open hands is to live without clinging, to receive and release with grace. It's to acknowledge that all we have is gift, that nothing is truly ours to possess. This posture fosters gratitude, humility, and a deep sense of connection to the Divine and to others.

In the end, mortality teaches. It confronts us with limits and calls us to wisdom we'd never seek on our own. It invites us into a deeper awareness of the present moment, into a fuller participation in the dance of life and death.

Some truths arrive sideways. They slip through windows left ajar, catching us unprepared. Truths that reshape us rarely arrive by invitation. Mortality has this kind of sideways power. It interrupts the ordered architecture of our beliefs, slips into the structure we've built around certainty, and rearranges the interior. At first, it feels like violation. Then it begins to feel like vision.

In spiritual formation, we often speak of mountaintop experiences, revelations that clarify, inspire, steady us. But the texts that endure rarely locate transformation on the heights. They locate it in exile. In caves. In wilderness. In belly of fish and darkened tomb. The holy does not always speak in clarity. Sometimes it arrives in disorientation.

Disorientation can become the shape of God's nearness. "God does not deal in confusion; the disruption comes when our illusions collapse under truth. When the familiar scaffolding collapses, when we lose the job, the health, the relationship, the belief, we reach for explanation. But explanation is often just the ego's attempt to reestablish control. What faith invites instead is participation. Show up to the unknowing. Dwell in the undoing.

Israel's forty years in the desert shaped a people not yet ready to be free. The time in the wilderness formed them. Time was needed to reshape them from travelers, into people capable of freedom. Their deliverance from Egypt was immediate. Their transformation into covenant-bearers was not. The desert taught them who they were. Mortality works in similar fashion. It strips us of immediacy, forces us to travel by slower wisdom.

When death comes close, when we witness it, brush against it, survive it, we often describe the world afterward as altered. The colors change. The air thickens. Conversations feel thinner or more piercing. This is not imagination. This is the nervous system registering reality without the filters of delusion. Mortality has peeled back the veil. We live differently when we remember we're temporary. And we worship differently too.

Much of modern spirituality is built on comfort. On the management of suffering, the explanation of hardship, the assurance that everything belongs. There is value in those consolations. But they do not always prepare us for the grave. What prepares us is encounter. Not answers. Presence. To sit with someone dying, not to rescue or explain, but simply to accompany them into mystery, is to practice reverence. To bury a loved one without resolving what they meant or how you'll survive without them is a kind of sacred apprenticeship. These are the places where theology stops performing and begins incarnating.

Hospice chaplains often frame resurrection as orientation, a way of attending to death rather than resolving it. Their belief emerges through proximity to the dying, formed in quiet rooms, beside final breaths, where nothing is explained but everything is seen. They speak of the soul's steadiness in the moment of departure, not universal, but unmistakable. Some resist. Some yield. But all, they say, cross into something language cannot follow. For those who serve at that threshold, belief becomes a decision. If there is a God worth loving, then that crossing must be held.

That is the kind of belief that survives the void. Certainty doesn't endure the void. Commitment does. Defense doesn't carry us through the dark. Devotion does. What remains is not what explains, but what stays. A willingness to keep showing up in the dark. In the cold. In the silence. And calling that worship.

Myth doesn't decode meaning. It reveals how to see. The stories that endure are not neat. They do not always resolve. They leave blood on the altar and questions unanswered. They leave the traveler altered. Gilgamesh cannot bring back Enkidu. Orpheus turns too soon. Job is silenced before he is restored. These are not failures of plot. They are invitations to fidelity. They show us how to go on without clarity. How to love without reward.

Christianity is often misread as a system of certainties. But its truest texture is paradox. A kingdom where the weak are strong. A savior who dies. A tomb that opens into bewilderment. The women who discover the resurrection do not rejoice at first. They run afraid. Resurrection is not a return to order. It is the beginning of something inconceivable. Resurrection doesn't restore what was. It initiates a world never seen before.

To let mortality shape us spiritually is to let that paradox take root. We stop demanding explanations. We stop waiting for the return of what was. We begin to watch for what wants to be born. And we do so with tenderness, not because we're unafraid, but because love matters more than protection.

I don't know what happens after this life ends. But I have seen what happens when we remember that this life ends. We slow down. We speak kinder. We forgive faster. We tell the truth more often. We quit postponing joy. We stop pretending that legacy is more important than intimacy. We show up as participants, letting the story unfold rather than forcing it to fit our script.

Sanctified disorientation isn't confusion; it's grace in unfamiliar form. It undoes what numbs us. It leaves the ache intact and enters it. Mortality doesn't conclude the spiritual life. It roots it. It gives the spirit something to grow in. Faith never promised escape. What it offers is companionship. A way to sit with death long enough to hear what it teaches. Long enough to be changed.

The mystics knew this. The saints carried it. The scriptures sing of it. And the grave, empty or not, still whispers: Wake up. Love better. Hold lightly. Begin again.

Chapter Ten

When the Clock Still Ticks for Others

Linear Time as Grief's Companion

It's strange how a clock can keep perfect rhythm in a room where something irreversible has occurred. The hour hand moves. The second hand ticks. Time doesn't pause, even when your life within it has.

I remember staring at the walls of her bedroom after my grandma died. The thermostat blinked 72°. Sunlight beamed through the window, casting a shadow across the floor. The air moved through the same vents it had the day before. Yet something had given way. And it wasn't loud. The rupture didn't tear time apart. It bent it, almost imperceptibly. A warping only the grieving can recognize.

Psychologists have long noted that grief distorts our experience of time. Moments stretch or vanish. Research on temporal processing shows that trauma alters how memories are stored. Emotionally intense events take up disproportionate neural space, which is why a single instant can feel endless, while entire days dissolve unnoticed (Stetson et al., 2007). This isn't metaphor. It's physiology. Under stress, the hippocampus falters. The prefrontal cortex, usually tasked with keeping sequence intact, struggles to make the days line up (Eagleman, 2009).

Time distortion is only part of the story. Grief also disrupts narrative. For those left living, time develops a fault line. There was before. Now there is after. This so-called "after" feels untethered. The person is gone. So is the plot that held them. Their story cut off mid-sentence. Yours moves forward without them. Something in that is dissonant.

Linear time demands continuation. Work resumes. Mail gets delivered. The body wants sleep, food, maintenance. Grief resists. Every part of you leans backward. You feel the pull to remain with the absence, to stand watch. In witness. Leaving might affirm what the soul still refuses to accept.

In physics, time's arrow points one way. Entropy assures that past states cannot be perfectly regained. Yet consciousness strains against this. Memory repeats. Ache repeats. The grieving repeat. Seconds continue in their clean succession. The mourner slips into a loop. Time spirals, stutters, reverses and advances at once.

This spiraling isn't error. It marks the place. It marks the one who is missed. Maybe it's even holy.

Ernest Becker, in The Denial of Death, writes that human beings are unique in their awareness of time and mortality, and that we build symbolic worlds to stand against disappearance (Becker, 1973). When grief is fresh, there are no symbols strong enough. Only the disorientation of continuing in a world that no longer waits.

Some mystics speak of a divine pause between death and resurrection, a holy silence echoing through the tomb. In that silence, something like time still occurs, but it is not linear. It does not progress. It dwells. The Orthodox tradition speaks of Christ's descent into Hades as accompaniment. In death, God joins the dead. In grief, then, we join God, as companions who refuse to abandon the darkness.

This is not consolation. It is a form of spiritual solidarity. It reframes grief as a location, a terrain where the soul learns to remain rather than escape. In the Psalms, lament is not weakness; it is declaration. To cry "How long, O Lord?" is to acknowledge time while refusing its tyranny (Psalm 13:1). Lament halts the machinery of progress and permits something older to surface: a communion that does not require answers.

Religions across cultures mirror this instinct. The Jewish practice of shiva marks seven days of structured stillness. Mourners sit low to the ground. Mirrors are covered. Visitors speak in hushed tones, if at all. Shiva is not passive. It grants shape to a time that has lost its form. It says: stay here. Be unmade. Let the rupture teach you something true. Only when nothing makes sense can the sacred finally interrupt.

In Christian liturgy, Holy Saturday is similarly quiet. It is the only day between crucifixion and resurrection, the only space in the Gospels where nothing happens. No miracles. No sermons. Just silence. And yet, that silence is held within the church calendar every year. It is not skipped. It is not an error. It is the hinge on which all theology turns.

Maybe this is why grief feels so spatial. It rearranges the coordinates of meaning. It insists we relearn orientation. This isn't a return. It's a way of walking through what now is. Jesus says, "Blessed are those who mourn, for they shall be comforted"

(Matthew 5:4). Comfort, in the Greek parakaleo, does not mean ease. It means to be called alongside. The blessing is not that mourning will end, but that it will be shared.

So we return to the still room. The clock ticks. The air moves. And we remain, not to fix or forget, but to remember how deeply love once took root. This, too, is resurrection: not reversal, but recognition. The dead are not lost to time. They are folded into it, and we, by grieving, are folded with them.

Perhaps Ecclesiastes understood this rhythm better than we do. "A time to weep... a time to laugh... a time to mourn... a time to dance" (Ecclesiastes 3:4). These aren't steps to follow. They describe what arrives when it arrives. Through surrender.

Time carries on. But the grieving don't walk its path in a line. They stall. They circle. They fall and rise. In that disarray, they hold the dead near by staying beside the stillness a little longer.

Reunion Across Dimensions

The longing to reunite with the dead is more than emotional. It speaks to the structure of our being. It doesn't arise only from missing someone. It comes from a deep intuition that love was never meant to vanish.

Even those who doubt the afterlife still find themselves whispering into the stillness, imagining someone listening from just beyond. Some part of us insists that separation should not be final.

Christian theology affirms this yearning but redirects it. In Christ, "death no longer has dominion" (Romans 6:9). Resurrection does not replay what was lost. It remakes life into something unbreakable (1 Corinthians 15:42–44). The hope is that we, and they, will be gathered into a union that no longer fractures.

This challenges how we think. Our minds frame reunion as sequence. I will die, and then I will find you. But if heaven is not measured in hours or waiting, then reunion may already hold its fullness in ways we cannot measure. C.S. Lewis, in The Great Divorce, calls heaven "the land where all moments are now."

In that view, reunion is not postponed. It is uncovered. A dimension we have not yet reached. Eternity holds what we experience as delay, and holds it differently.

Mystics have spoken this for centuries. Julian of Norwich recorded Christ's words, "All shall be well... and all manner of thing shall be well." She wasn't offering comfort for later. She was witnessing what exists beyond sequence. Reunion, for her, was never about waiting. It was about seeing what was already secure.

This strange truth finds echoes even in physics. Time, according to Einstein's relativity, is not universal. It shifts under gravity, bends with velocity. Events can unfold in different orders depending on the observer. There is no single clock keeping time for the cosmos. What if what we long for exists already, beyond the version of time we inhabit?

Myth, with its symbols, often places reunion in borderlands. Orpheus dares the underworld to reach Eurydice but fails when he turns back toward ordinary time. Christian resurrection offers no return to what was. It offers the beginning of what cannot decay. Mary Magdalene meets the risen Christ and tries to touch him. He says, "Do not cling to me..." (John 20:17). The reunion has begun, but not in the shape she expects. Presence is no longer measured by proximity.

This may be the clue.

Perhaps reunion is not the reappearance of what we once held. Perhaps it's the unveiling of what never ceased to be. Love rooted in God doesn't endure because we remember it. It endures because it was never bound by time.

This doesn't quiet grief. It doesn't restore the kitchen laughter, the familiar hands. It doesn't recreate what was. But it offers something fiercer. In the eternal, what is real does not dissolve. In Christ, those held in him are not scattered. They are gathered in a realm that remains hidden to those still walking within the veil.

So reunion may not be a final destination we reach. It may be something we discover the moment we step outside time.

But stepping outside time does not mean leaving behind identity. It does not mean becoming vague spirit or anonymous essence. The Christian hope is particular. It names and holds. Scripture speaks not only of resurrection, but of recognition. The transfigured Christ is still Jesus. He calls Mary by name. He invites Thomas to touch his side. The wounds remain, not as injuries, but as revelation.

This retention of identity is not sentiment. It is theological necessity. If resurrection forgets who we were, then it forgets what was redeemed. But if God gathers the whole of us, then memory, love, and relationship are not shed, they are restored in their incorruptible form.

This is why the early church resisted Platonic ideas of the soul's dissolution into the divine. They insisted on bodily resurrection, on new creation, on a heaven that is not escape but fulfillment. What began in the garden ends not in return, but in transformation: a new heaven, a new earth (Revelation 21:1). The story does not close by leaving the world. It culminates by making it whole.

And in that wholeness, reunion is more than meeting. It is recognition across transfigured being. In Paul's words, "Then I shall know fully, even as I am fully known" (1 Corinthians 13:12).

To be known is the deepest form of reunion. It restores what death appeared to fracture.

Even now, this knowing moves like a current beneath grief. When we ache for those who have gone, we do not merely long for presence. We long to be known again by them. We want to be seen in the way only they saw us. Their absence is not only the loss of their company. It is the loss of the reflection of ourselves that only they carried.

This is why eternity matters. It is not an endless extension of time. It is the state in which nothing true is ever lost.

In this vision, the communion of saints is not an idea. It is a reality hidden behind the veil of mortality. Those who have passed do not drift in some remote light. They are gathered in Christ, present in the mystery of the Church beyond borders of life and death. Their prayers join ours. Their songs continue. Their love, once embodied, now expands in ways we cannot chart but can still sense.

This is not a metaphor. It is the promise that undergirds Christian hope: that love is never wasted, that nothing entrusted to God is lost. What we call reunion may simply be the recovery of sight, the unveiling of what has always held us, even when we did not see it.

Letting Go, Letting Stay

I used to think letting go was the final act. The sign that the story had closed. A gentle ending wrapped in memory. Over time, I came to see something quieter, less certain: letting go does not end love. It changes where you find it.

We treat closure as a doorway meant to be crossed. The dead do not vanish like completed narratives. They remain, folded into a new kind of text. One without clear breaks. Their names still surface, sometimes as pain, sometimes as presence. Absence takes on contour. It settles beside us and stays.

Sometimes I think about my grandma. I remember how she used to sing, how music was just part of her. And I remember that eventually, she lost her song. I don't carry grief with me. I'm grateful for the time we had. And sometimes, I miss that. I suspect this is what Scripture gestures toward with "a great cloud of witnesses" (Hebrews 12:1), not an audience watching from elsewhere, but those whose lives have moved into a hidden fold of ours, still present in ways we can't quite measure.

Letting go is not rejection. It's a form of reverence. A loosening of our demand for visible form. For proof. For possession.

It isn't disloyal to stop gripping what cannot return. It takes faith to keep walking with empty hands, and fuller spirit. Grief becomes a ritual, one of remembering differently. It reshapes us, without demanding that we preserve the past like an artifact.

Jesus wept at Lazarus's tomb, knowing resurrection would follow (John 11:35). His tears weren't weakness. They affirmed that grief is part of love's fullness. That pain doesn't cancel faith, it reveals what matters. Maybe that's the call: to live beside the ache without resistance.

When we release what cannot be retrieved, something else can open. We begin to trust that those we love are not erased, just beyond reach. Not silent, only farther than our hearing can travel. We go on, living within the world grief has changed.

Death is often cast as life's opposite. Perhaps it stands as life's mirror. A shadow that sharpens our sight. A call to notice. To loosen our grip. To bow when beauty breaks something open in us.

Maybe eternity isn't waiting elsewhere. Maybe it runs beneath us now, glimpsed only in stillness.

So letting go does not erase. And holding on need not constrict.

To live fully is to carry the ache and the gift in the same hands. To be shaped by loss without being frozen in it. To become, through sorrow, someone more attuned to what remains.

And when our clocks still tick while theirs have stopped, we move forward with care. We don't rush. We don't flinch at the finish line.

We begin to see: time never held the meaning. Love did. And still does.

And if love still holds, then remembrance becomes more than an act of memory. It becomes a kind of stewardship. A way of carrying forward what no longer speaks aloud but still matters. In grief, we are entrusted with presence refracted. Our task is to preserve the radiance of what was, carried forward in a changed form.

This is why grief, though often seen as passive, carries within it a moral dimension. To mourn is to say, this mattered. This person, this bond, this laughter. It mattered enough to echo. Enough to break something open in us. In Jewish tradition, the Kaddish is not a prayer for the dead. It is a sanctification of God's name in the presence of death. It declares that even now, even here, we will bless the source of life. Not because we understand, but because we remain.

That act, of remaining, is itself sacred. To stand with loss in reverence, rather than falling into denial or despair, becomes its own spiritual practice. It aligns with the Christian vocation to witness. To keep vigil. To mark the passing with continuity.

This continuity extends beyond concept. In the sacramental imagination, every thread of reality touches the divine. Bread and wine become body and blood. Time and space bend under the weight of God's presence. If this is true, then so is the reverse: the ache of longing can become liturgy. The tear can become testimony. The silence after a name is spoken aloud can become a kind of prayer.

So we do not merely carry grief. We are shaped by it. And that shaping does not render us weaker. It renders us transparent. More able to see the contours of love where we once only saw form. This is not an argument against joy. It is a path into a deeper kind. One that holds sorrow without apology.

Christians are called to be resurrection people. But resurrection is not the avoidance of death. It is its transfiguration. The wounds remain. The love remains. And so do we, walking slowly, reverently, into a world now touched by both absence and glory.

To live in this tension is to live honestly. It is to say that loss resists resolution. Yet over time, it unfolds. And in that unfolding, something eternal draws near. Something that remains with pain and makes a home inside it. That is where Christ meets us, inside the ache itself, not beyond it.

Perhaps that is why the heart still lifts at remembered laughter. Why the ache does not nullify joy. Because the dead are not erased. They are gathered. And we, by loving them still, are gathered too. Into memory, yes, and into the deeper mystery that memory points toward.

CONCLUSION

The Space That Holds Us

We have traced the contours of absence, felt its weight in memory, in stillness, in the minutes that stretch impossibly long after a final breath. For all our language, the void remains intact. No closer. No clearer. Only more alive with questions.

This is not failure.

Some truths resist shape because they were never meant to be handled. They must be approached slowly, like fire in a darkened field. What happens between the last breath and whatever follows, if anything follows, has always remained more mystery than doctrine. Still, we return to it. Because it is sacred.

We do not live beside eternity. We live inside its tension. Each morning we rise into sequence, tethered to clocks, to stories, to cause and effect. We build meaning through rhythm, morning light, voices that return, footsteps we know by sound. When someone disappears from that rhythm, the world shifts. Time itself buckles. Their absence hollows a space and fractures continuity.

This is where the ache comes from. Dislocation. The coordinates have changed. Their name still echoes, but without return.

We mark time for both of us. We keep pace on behalf of someone who no longer walks within its frame.

What begins to heal, if healing is even the word, is presence. Attentiveness that sits through the silence. That keeps lighting candles even when no one speaks. If God is anywhere in this, it is in that ache, a God who listens, who remains present where no answers come. Holding it.

We build rituals for this. To stay close to what death touched. The prayer before sleep. The empty chair not moved. The daffodils planted beside a grave rarely visited but still remembered. These are not attempts to solve death. They allow us to remain inside its echo without being undone.

Perhaps that is what we were always meant to do.

Tend the mystery. Dwell near the void.

To live well is to live in rhythm with both presence and disappearance. To love is to agree, quietly, to be broken by time. And still, to keep loving. To let memory be incomplete. To let joy return in unpredictable shapes. To belong to the world in reverence.

And when the time comes, as it will, to cross the space we cannot see, may something in us remember what this was. The shape of breath. The warmth of a hand. The sound of someone else's footsteps in the kitchen. Not as proof of what waits, but as witness to what held us while we were here.

And maybe, if silence still listens, we will be held again.

Keeping the Questions Alive

Now that you've walked through the pages of *Into the Void*, you carry with you more than ideas. You carry presence. Wonder. A quiet permission to sit with what can't be named.

This book wasn't meant to give answers. It was meant to hold space.

If it has done that for you, there's something simple you can do to keep that space open for someone else.

By leaving your honest thoughts on Amazon, you help another soul, someone searching, someone grieving, someone questioning, find their way to this work.

They might not even know what they're looking for yet, but your voice might be the one that leads them here.

Thank you for helping keep the conversation alive.

The mystery endures because we continue to speak of it. You're helping me do just that.

Click or Scan here to leave your review on Amazon.

With gratitude,
Renae C. Linde

Also by Renae C. Linde: If You Were Moved by This Book, You May Also Appreciate...

When We Let Go

What happens when effort fades, ambition quiets, and responsibility dissolves into silence? *When We Let Go* traces the slow unraveling of personal agency in a culture that increasingly pathologizes striving. Equal parts critique and confession, this book examines the emotional and spiritual consequences of non-effort, quiet dependency, and inherited dysfunction, making it a powerful companion to *Into the Void* for readers drawn to existential inquiry.

→ *Cultural commentary, agency, grief by erosion*

ALSO BY RENAE C. LINDE

Fighting for Love

Some relationships thrive not in peace, but in tension. This book explores high-conflict intimacy, emotional friction, and the paradox of connection through resistance. If *Into the Void* compelled you with its psychological and theological tension, *Fighting for Love* will resonate with its emotional precision and refusal to flinch.
→ *Fearful-avoidant attachment, control vs. closeness, unresolved intensity*

Explore more titles at https://www.amazon.com/stores/author/B0DNY9VD34

Think Sharp

While *Into the Void* drifts into metaphysical and philosophical unknowns, *Think Sharp* anchors thought in clarity and logic. If you found yourself lost in mystery and now long for tools to ground your thinking, this guide to critical reasoning, emotional intelligence, and cognitive agility offers balance and recalibration.
→ *Decision-making, mental resilience, cognitive clarity*

REFERENCES

Active Christianity. (n.d.). *What does it mean to take up your cross daily?* Retrieved from https://activechristianity.org/what-does-it-mean-to-take-up-your-cross-daily

Aquinas, T. (1265–1274). *Summa Theologica* (First Part, Question 75).

Assmann, J. (2005). *Death and Salvation in Ancient Egypt.* Cornell University Press.

Augustine. (1991). *Confessions* (H. Chadwick, Trans.). Oxford University Press. (Original work published ca. 400)

Becker, E. (1973). *The denial of death.* Free Press.

Borjigin, J., Lee, U., Liu, T., Pal, D., Huff, S., Klarr, D., ... & Mashour, G. A. (2013). *Surge of neurophysiological coherence and connectivity in the dying brain.* Proceedings of the National Academy of Sciences, 110(35), 14432–14437. https://doi.org/10.1073/pnas.1308285110

Brayne, S., Farnham, C., &Fenwick, P. (2011). *Nearing death awareness: A guide to the language, visions, and dreams of the dying.* American Journal of Hospice and Palliative Medicine, 28(1), 7–15. https://doi.org/10.1177/1049909110372600

Catholic Digest. (n.d.). *Memento Mori*. Retrieved from https://www.catholicdigest.com/amp/faith/spirituality/memento-mori/

Dawkins, R. (1976). *The selfish gene.* Oxford University Press.

Eagleman, D. (2009). *Sum: Forty Tales from the Afterlives.* Pantheon.

Eagleman, D. (2011). *Incognito: The Secret Lives of the Brain.* Pantheon Books.

Einstein, A. (1955). *Letter to the family of Michele Besso*, March 1955.

Faulkner, R. O. (2005). *The Ancient Egyptian Book of the Dead* (C. Andrews, Ed.). University of Texas Press.

Fremantle, F., & Trungpa, C.(2003). *The Tibetan Book of the Dead: The Great Liberation Through Hearing in the Bardo* (R. Thurman, Pref.). Shambhala Publications.

Greene, B. (2004). *The fabric of the cosmos: Space, time, and the texture of reality.* Alfred A. Knopf.

Gregory of Nyssa. (1993). *On the soul and the resurrection* (C. R. H. Mackintosh, Trans.). St. Vladimir's Seminary Press. (Original work published ca. 4th century)

Hawking, S. (2001). *The universe in a nutshell.* Bantam Books.

Heidegger, M. (1995). *The fundamental concepts of metaphysics: World, finitude, solitude* (W. McNeill & N. Walker, Trans.). Indiana University Press. (Original work published 1929)

Heschel, A. J. (1955). God in search of man: A philosophy of Judaism. Farrar, Straus and Giroux.

Hoffman, D. D. (2019). *The case against reality: Why evolution hid the truth from our eyes.* W. W. Norton & Company.

Holy Bible, New Revised Standard Version. (1989). Division of Christian Education of the National Council of the Churches of Christ in the United States of America.

Holy Bible. (1000 BCE - 90 CE/2001). English Standard Version. *Genesis 1:2; Genesis 1:5; Genesis 3:19; Genesis 11:4; Exodus 33:23; 2 Kings 2:11; Job 14:1–3; Job 38:4; Psalm 39:5 – 6; Psalm 90:4; Psalm 115:17; Psalm 139:6, 13; Ecclesiastes 3:11; Isaiah 26:19; Isaiah 49:15 – 16; ; Isaiah 65:17; Nehemiah 8:10; Matthew 10:39; Matthew 16:25; Matthew 17:2; Matthew 27:46; Luke 1:38; Luke 9:23, 29; Luke 22:19, 44; John 11:35; John 15:11; John 20:17; Romans 6:9; 1 Corinthians 13:8, 12; 1 Corinthians 15:14, 44, 52, 53; 2 Corinthians 5:2, 8; 1 Thessalonians 5:2; Philippians 2:7; Hebrews 12:1; James 4:14; 2 Peter 3:8; 1 John 4:8; Revelation 8:1; Revelation 20:12; Revelation 21:1, 5; Revelation 22:5.* Crossway.

Holy Qur'an. (n.d.). *Surah An-Nahl 16:77*. Retrieved fromhttps://quran.com/16/77

Julian of Norwich. (1998). *Revelations of divine love* (E. Spearing, Trans.). Penguin Books. (Original work published ca. 1395)

Kalanithi, P. (2016). *When breath becomes air*. Random House.

Langdell, T. (2018). Kenosis: Christian Self-Emptying Meditation. Christ Way Press.

Lewis, C. S. (1945). *The great divorce*. Harper One.

Lewis, C. S. (1952). *Mere Christianity*. Harper One.

Locke, J. (1690). *An Essay Concerning Human Understanding*. London: T. Basset.

Mark, J. J. (2011). Inanna's Descent: A Sumerian Tale of Injustice. World History Encyclopedia. https://www.worldhistory.org/article/215/inannas-descent-a-sumerian-tale-of-injustice/

Martial, C., Cassol, H., Charland-Verville, V., Pallavicini, C., & Laureys, S. (2021). *Near-death experiences as a probe to explore (dis)connected consciousness.* Trends in Cognitive Sciences, 25(11), 803–816. https://doi.org/10.1016/j.tics.2021.06.014

McGrew, W. F., Zhang, X., Fasano, R. J., Schäffer, S. A., Beloy, K., Nicolodi, D., ... & Ludlow, A. D. (2018). *Atomic clock performance beyond the geodetic limit.* arXiv preprint arXiv:1807.11282.

Meister Eckhart. (c. 1300/2009). Selected writings (O. Davies, Trans.). Penguin Classics.

Monks of Norcia. (n.d.). *Death before our eyes.* Retrieved from https://en.nursia.org/blog/death-before-our-eyes

Montag, C., Sindermann, C., Becker, B., & Panksepp, J. (2019). *Digital phenotyping in psychological and medical sciences: A reflection about necessary prerequisites to reduce harm and increase benefits.* Current Opinion in Psychology, 36, 19–24. https://doi.org/10.1016/j.copsyc.2020.04.007

Morris, D. (2004). *The Enuma Elish: The Babylonian creation epic.* In Myths from Mesopotamia: Creation, the Flood, Gilgamesh, and Others (S. Dalley, Trans., pp. 228–277). Oxford University Press.

Nagel, E., & Newman, J. R. (2001). *Gödel's proof.* New York University Press.

National Institute of Standards and Technology. (n.d.). *Time in physics.* Retrieved from https://en.wikipedia.org/wiki/Time_in_physics

New Revised Standard Version Bible. (1989). *2 Kings 2:11; Matthew 17:2.* Division of Christian Education of the National Council of the Churches of Christ in the United States of America.

Nussbaum, M. C. (2001). *The Fragility of Goodness: Luck and Ethics in Greek Tragedy and Philosophy.* Cambridge University Press.

Plotinus. (1991). *The Enneads* (S. MacKenna, Trans.). Penguin Classics. (Original work ca. 250 CE)

Rahula, W. (1974). *What the Buddha Taught.* Grove Press.

Rohr, R. (2017). Self-Emptying and Kenosis: The Pattern of Reality. Center for Action and Contemplation. https://cac.org/daily-meditations/self-emptying-and-kenosis-the-pattern-of-reality-2017-03-05/

Rosenblum, B., & Kuttner, F.(2011). *Quantum Enigma: Physics Encounters Consciousness (2nd ed.)*. Oxford University Press.

Rovelli, C. (2018). *The order of time*. Riverhead Books.

Rohr, R. (2013). *Immortal Diamond: The Search for Our True Self*. Jossey-Bass.

Sacks, J. (2003). *The Dignity of Difference: How to Avoid the Clash of Civilizations*. Continuum.

Stetson, C., Fiesta, M. P., &Eagleman, D. M. (2007). *Does time really slow down during a frightening event?* PLoS ONE, 2(12), e1295. https://doi.org/10.1371/journal.pone.0001295

Teresa of Ávila. (c. 1577/2004). *The interior castle* (M. Starr, Trans.). Riverhead Books.

Wackermann, J., Pütz, P., Büchi, S., Strauch, I., & Allefeld, C. (2008). *Ganzfeld-induced hallucinatory experience, its phenomenology and cerebral electrophysiology*. Cortex, 44(10),1364–1378. https://doi.org/10.1016/j.cortex.2007.05.003

Wikipedia contributors. (n.d.). *Unit of time*. In Wikipedia, The Free Encyclopedia. Retrieved fromhttps://en.wikipedia.org/wiki/Unit_of_time

World History Encyclopedia. (n.d.). *Inanna's Descent: A Sumerian Tale of Injustice*. Retrieved from https://www.worldhistory.org/article/215/inannas-descent-a-sumerian-tale-of-injustice/

Wright, N. T. (2008). Surprised by hope: Rethinking heaven, the resurrection, and the mission of the church. HarperOne.

Yalom, I. D. (2008). *Staring at the Sun: Overcoming the Terror of Death*. Jossey-Bass.

www.ingramcontent.com/pod-product-compliance
Lightning Source LLC
Chambersburg PA
CBHW030452100526
44580CB00006B/93/J